FORGIVENESS

How difficult it is!

A.P. Parashar

F-2/16, Ansari Road, Daryaganj, New Delhi-110002
E-mail: info@unicornbooks.in • Website: www.unicornbooks.in
☎ 011-23275434, 23262683, 23250704

Branch : Mumbai
23-25, Zaoba Wadi, Thakurdwar, Mumbai-400002
☎ 022-22010941, 022-22053387
E-mail: rapidex@bom5.vsnl.net.in

ISBN: 978-81-7806-400-0

Edition: 2018

Printed at : *Thomson Press (India) Ltd.*

Preface

Once while I was visiting my children in US, I happened to go to Angleton Library in Angleton town, around forty miles away from Houston in Texas towards the sea. Going through different types of magazines and journals, I happened to look at July 2014 Reader's Digest, American Version. While turning the pages of the Digest, I came across an interesting article written by the Archbishop Emeritus Desmond Tutu who also won the Nobel Peace Prize in 1984. The article was about '**Forgiveness**' titled "**Why We Forgive?**". I was deeply moved by reading it as things mentioned in it were the ones that usually happen in people's life and go on disturbing them most of the time.

I think Archbishop Desmond Tutu was right that if one remained in the old painful memories, one would feel wanting to hurt the person who had inflicted pain or injury on you in some manner. Any time when you recall the story or if the scene comes across your imagination, you are likely to be distressed as your mind gets filled in with the feelings of remorse and anguish. You may also strongly feel to hurt back the person who has inflicted all that pain. Even if you try to forget the situation, it goes on reappearing in your mind again and again in spite of your constantly efforts to forget it. How difficult the process of forgetting or forgiving truly is? Even if many years have gone, the old memories go on hurting and causing pain each time they come back to your memory.

Thus, every kind of injury, whether old or new, is a kind of unhealed wound. You strongly feel that what was done to you was wrong or unfair. The moment that feeling comes back to your mind you, get outraged. It is also quite normal to hurt back when you have been hurt. However, hurting back never satisfies. On the contrary it gives fresh pain and your anguish is doubled. When we hurt back, we usually think that it would satisfy us. But it does not. Retaliation may give us only momentary relief, but soon the sad feelings overtake and we are filled in with the usual pain once again.

Archbishop Tutu recommends that the only way to get healing and peace is to forgive the person who has inflicted pain. That is the only way to get comfort. Until we forgive, we stay locked in our pain and consequently go on locked out of the possibility of getting healed and become free. As a result, we also stay out of the possibility of being at peace. Without forgiving, we stay fastened to the person who has harmed us and the chins of bitterness go on trapping us. So, forgiving is necessary, for without that we would never experience any comfort or peace. When we forgive others we take back control of our own fate and feelings. That is the only way to get healed, feel happy and get redeemed.

A.P. Parashar
Angleton, Texas,
1st June, 2016

Contents

About the Author

Prof. Ambika Prasad Parashar after completing his education, joined the Department of Education in Rajasthan State, where he worked for fifteen years as Lecturer in English. He then left for abroad. After serving at various places at abroad, including thirteen years at Sokoto University in Nigeria. He retired as Professor and Head of Education Department at the Faculty of Education, IASE, Vidyabhawan Udaipur. He also visited Willamette University at Salem, Oregon, USA, as a Visiting Scholar for one year.

He has been actively engaged in writing inspirational books for the last forty years that includes some textbooks of B.Ed. and M.Ed. as well. In all so far he has more than forty-eight books to his credit. He has completed five research projects funded by various universities, and published nearly 98 articles in India and abroad in International Journals. Some of his noted books are: **Meaning to Know Thyself, Concept of Freedom, Seeking Right Mindfulness, Meera—The Divine Incarnate, Happiness is Divine, Transcending Yourself, The Path of Dharma, Unparalleled Love, History of Educational Philosophy, Teaching of English, Teaching & Learning Process** and several others. Out of these, a couple of books have also been published in USA.

Prof. Parashar is still actively busy in writing books and with educational activities that include guiding research students in the field of his interest. He also visits, quite often, different Universities in Rajasthan as well as in the northern states to examine Ph.D. students and to conduct their viva. He has also been editing an Educational Journal, named **"Chatena, International Journal of Education"**, for the last eight years.

1

Dwelling in Painful Memories

When we are hurt, we normally don't forgive people who have offended us in some way. We go on remembering those incidents and occasions that brought us disgrace, insults and filled our hearts with woeful thoughts. It is a part of human nature to retaliate to such situations or occasions overtly or silently as the amount of remorse and displeasure has been immense. I have witnessed several incidents when either I was personally hurt or when someone else, very close to me, was hurt by any person. It was always a terrible situation and retaliation was quite usual. However, one cannot retaliate at all the occasions. Therefore, the feelings of sadness are bound to come to one's memory whenever those feelings occupy one's mind. It is a bad situation when one is unable to forgive or forget all that pain inflicted by someone.

Something of that nature was reported by the Archbishop Emeritus Desmond Tutu in his book "**The Book of Forgiveness**", which later on was condensed in the form of an article relating Forgiveness, and was published in the Reader's Digest. The following few lines from the Digest are being reproduced hereunder for the readers' reference.

"There were so many nights when I, as a young boy, had to watch helplessly as my father verbally and physically abused my mother. I can still recall the smell of alcohol, see the fear in my mother's eyes, and feel the hopeless despair that comes when we see people we love hurting each other in incomprehensible ways........."

Exactly such situations in different ways and manner may happen in one's own family or someone else's family which is very close to you. You simply go on helplessly watching things happening. Several such scenes usually leave an unpleasant picture in our minds. How disdainful it would be when a son starts attempting to thresh his own father or mother as they are unable to fulfill his demands or financial needs? Just two days back, I watched on television that how a daughter used to beat her old mother bitterly. The cries of the old lady were distinctly heard by the neighbours but none dare to interfere or try to save the old lady from the beatings of her own daughter, though many of them did feel terribly bad at the situation happening repeatedly almost every evening.

The Archbishop Tutu's had similar experiences in his own life when his father would beat his mother terribly. He writes:

"I would not wish that experience on anyone, especially not a child. If I dwell in those memories, I can feel myself wanting to hurt my father back, in the same way he hurt my mother and in ways of which I was incapable as a small boy. I see my mother's face and see this gentle human being whom I loved so much and who did nothing to deserve the pain inflicted upon her." He adds further:

"When I recall this story, I realize how difficult the process of forgiving truly is. Intellectually, I knew my father caused pain because he was in pain. Spiritually, I know my faith tells me my father deserves to be forgiven as God forgives us all. But it is still difficult. The traumas we have witnessed or experienced live in our memories. Even years later they can cause us fresh pain each time we recall them."

So many real stories or true happenings of that nature are there close to my memory. I have witnessed them very closely as some of those, who created the unpalatable bitter scenes, were very close to me. When someone was beaten bitterly for none of his/her fault, was a great agony to me to watch all that happening. The oppressed lady, crying bitterly for help, but none of us who were able to interfere at the scene, could do anything as usually the person who attacked his wife, would often lock the doors of his room from inside and started beating her bitterly. At times he would undress her and beat her with a stick. It was discovered only when the incidence was over. One could hear clearly every sound of the beating by a wooden stick as it threshed loudly on the lady's body. The sound of each strike was not only heard from outside, but also the lady's instant shrieks disclosed it. Our shouting to stop all that from outside would result in futile. The person would go on beating her for a few minutes until she would fell on the ground. Then he often poured out filthy abuses and after a few minutes opened the door. We could see her laying on the ground, moaning with pain and crying bitterly, more on account of the hurt and insult inflicted to her tender feelings.

One can imagine the pathos of the disgraced lady as well as the amount of sadness that would usually fill the hearts of all those who witnessed such atrocities being done to someone in her own house where she was brought in gracefully after the marriage. It all happened several times for many years right in the presence of a few near relatives, including the small two children that she had given birth a few years back. What an agony! Its memory often fills my heart with remorse and astonishment that someone who apparently loved his wife so much, could beat her so bitterly that after the happening she would go on crying for hours. And then remembering that her two children would be hungry, she would get up and start doing her routine household work as if nothing had happened. But did she really forget all what had happened to her only few minutes ago? Perhaps not! On the contrary, whenever all that would come back to her memory, she must have felt retaliating against the man. She could not do anything of that nature at that time on account of her own limitedness and dependency on him. It went on and on until 25 years were spent with that man and when the children grew young, completed their education and were engaged in fruitful jobs.

Being a very close member of the family, once as I was visiting the family again as usual at some occasion, some kind of discussions erupted between the younger son and the father. The eldest son had left for market at that occasion to buy some necessary requirements for the family. Unfortunately, the discussions went on and on and at one point, the father and the son exchanged heated dialogues which were unpalatable and usually not heard in a respectable family. As the heated discussions continued further, the son got up from his seat and rushed towards his father to thresh him. The mother, standing quite nigh, looked towards the son expecting something to happen. Her eyes obviously seemed to be reflecting the feelings of revenge. As the boy raised his hand to beat the father, I immediately held the boy's raised hand. It was an odd situation, especially to someone like me, who being so close to the family, was present at that odd occasion.

However, heated and abusive discussions continued for quite long. The wife of the man gradually joined hands with her son against her husband and slowly incited the boy to thresh him. Well, as I was also there at that moment, I checked the boy and his mother to do all that and advised them not to do any such thing at all.

After a while the eldest son also came back from the market. By then much had been settled and verbal discussions almost ended. All what had happened was not only painful but also unbearable. Only then I was reminded of the old things which had happened years back several times in that house. Most people don't forget the insults at all and whenever they get a chance to take revenge, they do so. But it is also true that revenge never satisfies us and generates more dissatisfaction. Consequently, the odd feelings go on harbouring in the mind, often disturbing the heart and inciting repeatedly to act violently again and again. I have already reproduced the Archbishop's few lines earlier, saying that 'how difficult the process of forgiving truly is'. Even years afterwards, such instances and happenings, can cause pain and wild feelings each time we recall them. How can that lady who was beaten bitterly several times for 20 to 25 years, could easily forget all that?

Therefore, it is perfectly normal to want to hurt back when you have been hurt several times. So, the reactions of the lady and the son were not abnormal. However, slapping someone after you are slapped could look normal. But it is not normal. It does not lessen the pain, suffering and the hurt inflicted by someone. Retaliation may give, at best, simply momentary relief from our hurt feelings. But it is not the right way to extinguish the pain that have been lurking inside you for so long. Desmond Tutu discovered all that after a long time. That too he could do so as he continued leading a pious life and devoted his time to help people who were in distress.

First of all the Bishop Tutu tried to redeem his own pain that had been cradling in his bosom for so long. After a long thought and when he had acquired a rich experience in life by walking steadily for years on the road leading to God's House, he discovered something very amazing. When some kind of suffering is going on in one's heart and mind on account of previous insult and hurt, the right way is not retaliation. Retaliation may give us, at best, only momentary satisfaction from our suffering. The only way to attain peace and get healed is to forgive. Desmond Tutu unfolds, "Until we can forgive, we remain locked in our pain and locked out of the possibility of experiencing healing and freedom, locked out of the possibility of being at peace. Without forgiveness, we remain tethered to the person who harmed us."

Well, all such ideas are great for only those who like to forgive or need to be forgiven, but not for those who never think in that direction. Most people don't like to forgive and consequently, they go on harbouring the ills that have been done to them by someone in the past. It is nothing abnormal. It is quite natural to retaliate when surrounded with danger. Truly speaking, if someone is insulted by abuses or publicly beatings, it is quite natural to retaliate against that person. We have already related a real story of a woman, who was beaten brutally by her husband. It was therefore, quite natural for the woman to retaliate against her man when she got a chance to do so.

Our old legends, *Ramayana* and *Mahabharata* also contain such stories which most people take to be true. There would have never been a battle between Shri Ram and Ravana, if Laxman, the younger brother of Shri Ram, had not cut the nose of Surpenkhan. In fact, it was also not Laxhman's fault to cut her nose, but Surpenkhan just invited all that by insisting upon Shri Ram to marry her. Ram's constant refusal to do so, as well as, the plea that he was already married, did not mean anything to Surpenkhan, the female devil and the sister of Ravana. After her nose was cut off, she invoked Ravan's vengeance against Sri Rama and forced him to lift Sita, the wife of Shri Rama, from the Panchwati, the forest abode of the three, Shri Ram, Laxhman and Sita. As Surpenkhan's nose was cut off, it was quite natural for her to revolt against Shri Ram and Laxhman. Her abhorrence against Shri Rama at his refusal to marry her, became the cause of her constant hatred against him. Consequently, she filled Ravan's heart with vengeance. Thus, all that ultimately became the cause of Ravana's ruin and Lanka's destruction.

The story of *Mahabharat* is also based on such facts which contain hatred and insults against Pandavas by Kauravas. Most of the Indians as well as people abroad who have read *Mahabharat* know how all that happened. If Pandavas had not lost Dropadi, their wife, in gambling and if Kauravs had not tried to undress Dropadi in public after winning her in the gamble, no war would have taken place between Kauravas and Pandavas. It is another legendry story that unfolds insults on others publicly and by committing social crime and atrocity against their own nearest cousins. Like Ravana, all the Kauravs were also destroyed. Their feeling of taking revenge against their own brothers, resulted in their own devastation. Thus, though feeling of revenge is so natural and usually people don't think twice and just go ahead to indulge in hurting the person who has been the cause of the trouble. But it certainly has ill effects and takes its toll.

Is there any way to get rid of the terrible feelings that incite revenge? Is there a way to subside your irritating mood against one who has hurt you? Yes, certainly there are always ways to redeem matters that look difficult to be converted. One way is the one that the Archbishop has suggested. It is 'Forgiveness'. Try forgiving him/her who has hurt you. Yet, there is another way that Jiddu Krishnamurti has unfolded. It is 'just try emptying your mind from every kind of thought.' We will discuss both of them at the appropriate place in the book, but right now we would like to proceed further to discuss the important issue 'It is perfectly normal wanting to hurt back, when you are hurt. Why should you not be outraged when you are hurt?'

2

It is Perfectly Normal Wanting to Hurt Back

It is just normal as well as a natural feeling to retaliate against someone who has miffed you. Even if someone speaks loudly in a tone which is not natural/normal to respond, it can create problems and many a times we have witnessed skirmishes developing only on very small matters, like when someone does not respond to a call or retorts with a louder tone.

A simple example of this sort would be that when someone asks his 'boy' (servant) to bring a glass of water for him and if he delays in bringing it when he was asked twice, the master may get annoyed and could say, 'Hey, don't you listen to me? How many times would I ask you to bring me a glass of water?' The servant, being busy in some other household work, could neither respond to the master orally nor bring the glass of water. But when he gets another call, the boy gets agitated and responds in a bit louder voice, "Yes, I am bringing it soon, sir." "But how soon will you bring it? How many years will you take to bring a glass of water? I have been calling you for such a long-time and you are not responding at all."

When the boy brings water after some time, he gets a good thresh and warning as well and asked not to repeat such things in future. Though no further words were exchanged, the boy was made aware of the consequences for not responding to the master's call at once. At such occasions simply ***complexes work on both sides***. Let us examine the situation from that point of view.

How Complexes Work!

If we examine the above situation closely, we can easily expand it in the following way:

1. The master, though thirsty, calls the boy to bring him water with the right of being the master and superior to him.
2. The boy, though in a subordinate position, takes a few seconds in not responding as he was obviously busy in some other tasks that also belonged to the master's household. He thought that he could give some excuses for the delay. But he could not as ***the ego*** of his master was greatly inflated.

The boy, not intentionally, but due to his circumstances, got delayed but he got a kind of hidden warning not to repeat the act again (or he would be released of his duties). If we look at the above situation closely, we simply find that it is just a very small matter which the master could have avoided easily but his ego is so much inflated that he cannot accept any insolence on the part of his servant, though the servant may or not be insolent. Therefore, complexes go on working in life and become the cause of our problems, creating gradually shocking situations which end up in devastations.

Now, think about the same situation a little more from a different angle.

The servant after bringing the glass of water tells the master very politely that 'he was too busy with some important work in the kitchen so the delay was caused.' The master being kind and possessing a non-egoistic nature, tells him, "OK, just forget it." It gives relief to both, the servant as well as the master. No hidden warnings were involved. On the contrary more love and respect for each other was overtly displayed. But we normally don't do so as we usually suffer from ego that goes on cradling in our hearts and minds.

At this juncture I am reminded of a few lines from the Great Buddha's Dhammapada, which is one of the most beloved and accessible masterpieces from early Buddhist texts. It unfolds how if a person speaks with evil thoughts, pain would come to him in different ways:

All that we are is the result of what we have thought: it is founded on our thoughts, it is made up of our thoughts. If a man speak or acts with an evil thought, pain follows him, as the wheel follows the foot of the ox that draws the carriage.

However, if we change our way of thinking and as a result speaks to others, the panorama of life would change by itself The Dhammapada describes:

All what we are is the result of what we have thought: it is founded on our thoughts, it is made up of our thoughts. If a man speaks or acts with pure thought, happiness follows him, like a shadow that never leaves.

Thus, unwanted thoughts, often destroy one's peace and go on invading the mind. Consequently, the person, who cradles such thoughts, goes on and on harping on the same tune, thinking how he should take revenge against someone who said a few hurting words. The ***main culprit is the inbuilt ego,*** which never leaves one's company. Whatever situation there may be, one is usually apprised with the feeling of ego, which makes him/her move in a particular direction. If the master goes on thinking that since he is the master, he must immediately be obeyed by the servant, trouble will follow. Because he did not consider at all in what situation will the household servant would be. His ego has filled in him a kind of self-pride which forces him to act at that occasion. Such acts, which are backed simply by ego and not done by reasonable thoughts, are generally followed by troubles and usually bring remorse.

Let us explain it further by another simple example. Sometimes, two close friends may start discussing about the availability of a certain item in a particular shop that both of them often visits. Gradually, they come to a point that the particular item they are talking about is available in the shop or not available. One of them says with great confidence that it is available but the other goes on rejecting the idea and loudly condemns it. In fact, it is not an issue to discuss as when next they visit the shop, they can check about its availability there. Or if it is something which is needed by either of them immediately, they can instantly proceed to the shop and check it and buy it if available. But instead of doing something like that, they go on discussing about its availability in the shop. Ultimately and gradually they come to a point when the discussion is turned into hot exchanges, blaming each other that they don't trust each other so why continue any friendship further. And as soon as this idea tracks through their minds, they get separated. What an agony! Thus, at times impractical things may be the cause of breaking one's bonds which had been built after a long time.

Similarly, at times two close friends go on discussing about another (third) friend's sincerity and honesty. He is quite close to both of them. One of them trusts that friend too much but the other one has some reservations about him. Gradually, after some time, the easy going talks get converted into furious discussions, resulting in breaking the old bonds that were built after a long time. What works behind all such breaks and breaches in the old friendships? Often it is just a futile discourse. Apparently it has no meaning, but on account of ego, an ordinary situation reaches a point when close friends break their old bonds and get separated. Now, what is that something which has been working behind that ego? There is some thought or belief which always works when such situations arise. It is in fact a personal thought attached to the self of people and that thought does not permit them to go beyond it. That thought is 'I am always right.'

I am Always Right

Ego is good as far as it pushes people to go ahead and to work in a certain direction, but it can be troublesome, if it leads a person to a wrong direction. The right direction can only be followed if good thoughts accompany ego. Otherwise it may lead a person to an erroneous path. Sometimes, ego is backed with the thought that 'I am always right.' which quite often leads one to a wrong direction. Several people often become prey to this sort of thinking. They usually start giving their opinions in every matter whether it is connected with them or not. No one can always be right in all matters all the time. Is it not desirable that others should also be given a chance to speak and say whatever they think appropriate?

Thus, the thought, "I am always right" has a long chain of ill thoughts, like jealousy, hatred, unnecessary comparison of things etc., which lead to troubles and bestow problems. In fact, it is the 'thought' which is the main cause of troubles. Ill thought of any kind leads one to disasters and often brings problems. I will like to produce a few more lines from the Dhammapada to support how ill-thoughts lead one to a wrong direction.

"He abused me, he beat me, he defeated me,
he robbed me"---in those who harbour such
thoughts, hatred will never cease."

It is a basic fact that hatred never ceases by hatred at any time. It can stop only by love. It is an old rule which still governs people's thinking. Desmond Tutu therefore, rightly reflected: "retaliation gives, at best, only momentary respite from our emotional pain. The only way to experience healing and peace is to forgive." But we never realize it and go on cradling ill thoughts which look so natural that anyone can become prey of such thoughts, especially in difficult circumstances.

Identify your Hatred

If one can identify the thoughts of hatred blooming within one's mind and heart, life would be much easier than it looks at times, especially when one is backed by the feelings of hatred. I am reminded at this juncture a very old and real story from past history which unfolds about hatred contained by the younger brother for his own elder one for quite a long time.

Long back, Maharana Pratap, the ruler of Mewar State in Rajasthan in India, during 16th century, fought bravely against the Mughal Emperor, Akbar. Nearly all of Pratap's fellow Rajput chiefs had meanwhile entered into the vassalage of the Mughals. Even Pratap's own brothers, Shakti Singh, out of jealousy and hatred, served the Mughal Emperor along with other chieftains.

In the Battle of Haldighati fought against the Mughal Emperor Akbar, Maharana Pratap and his forces were heavily outnumbered by the Mughals. In order to change the odds to his side, Pratap mounted on his horse Chetak, fought very bravely. But Chetak's leg got deeply wounded in the process of the attack. Pratap also got injured and fell unconscious on the ground for some time due to a heavy blow by an elephant. When Rana came back to his senses, he managed to take a big leap and mounted on the injured horse Chetak. Though Chetak could hold him for some time but ultimately succumbed to his injuries. Maharana Pratap was heartbroken at the demise of his best friend Chetak. Meanwhile, when Pratap was mourning Chetak's death and was totally devoid of any kind assistance, his brother Shakti Singh, who had defected towards the Mughals out of jealousy and hatred, gave his horse to Pratap so that he could manage to escape from the Mughal soldiers who were chasing him gradually. It is just a true tale of two human beings who were real brothers, had departed for years due to the feelings of hatred, but when hatred was controlled and subsided, love prevailed and all became good.

Many a times, most people don't recognise the base feelings thriving within their hearts on account of jealousy or hatred and they go on injuring the persons against whom such injurious feelings are thrived. But if one's love overpowers those feelings, hatred will be subdued and peace will prevail.

Conceive the Truth out of Untruth

It is usual that most people don't conceive the truth out of prevailing untruth and go on harming others for their own benefits as well as on account of the feelings of dislike for others. Mind it, that dislike and hatred are slightly different from each other. In dislike strong feelings of hatred are not implicit. The moment one possesses dislike for someone, ill feelings for that person may gradually filter through one's mind and he/she would go on thinking only bad things about others. Thus, hatred grows out of dislike. Buddha has very appropriately reflected about it. He unfolds:

As rain breaks through an ill-thatched house,
passion will break through an unreflecting mind.

But if the person is judicious and does not permit ill thoughts to creep in, all will go smoothly.

As rain does not break through a well-thatched
house, passion will not break through,
a well reflected mind.

Usually, it does not happen so. I am in the know of someone, a lady, who usually goes on conceiving only wrong things about others and consequently reflects bad opinion about them when some incidence happens even inadvertently. I would like to provide an examples of her reflections she usually makes at the time when something happens.

Once while I was sitting with her along with her family, a visitor came to see them. Gradually, as we all involved in casual talks and gossips, the lady got up and in a few moments brought tea and refreshment for all of us. While we were enjoying our tea, one of the person's tooth broke down as he was munching some hard crackers. The person gradually took his broken tooth out and showing it to all of us, commented, "Oh, I broke my tooth. I got it fixed a few months back only." Without knowing the history of the person's teeth, the lady abruptly commented, "Oh, these days doctors know nothing about their jobs." The truth was that the doctor tried hard to fix it twice in two years and also did route canalling but as nothing much was left out on the top of the broken teeth to fix and repair it, finally it gave way and broke out. This was revealed by the person himself sometime after the incidence took place. But the lady just commented as her thinking, most of the time, is surrounded by negative ideas only.

Therefore, if dislike for others exists in your mind, you are bound to hurt others. Thinking that you are always right without recognising your own negative thoughts, you are likely to go on a wrong path and hurt others unknowingly. It is therefore, imperative that you must identify your down dislikes and hatred against others and try hard to subside the ill thoughts before they flare up in the mind, so that no ill reflections are poured out.

It is also very necessary that you should go on trying to conceive the truth out of the untruth. When police tries to learn about a theft case or when someone is injured or murdered, it (if it is honest) goes on inquiring from different people several times about the incidence before coming to any conclusion. Even then it is not necessary that right results could be reached. The inquiry goes on and on until the right results are reached. In the same manner, we all need to go on thinking correctly before coming to any conclusion. Results drawn hurriedly, or reflections made without properly thinking, may often lead us to an erroneous direction. We provide another real example at this point. It will highlight our views relating ***erroneous thinking backed by ego.***

How Ego Distorts Relationships

A newly married couple was enjoying their lives most lovingly and peacefully. Both were working in a big town in India just after getting married as both got jobs related to their education and experience. The boy was already working in the same town after completing his education from abroad and the girl joined him after they were married. Hardly a few days had passed that the mother of the boy came to visit them and to know how they were leading their lives. After staying for a couple days with her son, the lady realized that the couple did not have enough of crockery and certain utensils that they needed for day-to-day household use. She went to the market and bought all those needed things in their house.

All went very well for a few days but one evening, suddenly some sort of discussions erupted about one of girl's relatives. The mother-in-law (mother of the boy) was of the opinion that the particular person about whom they were talking, was not a good person, while the daughter-in-law insisted that it was not so. He was a good man. It is quite customary at certain places to talk about anyone in one's absence and deduce any results about someone's conduct. So, the mother-in-law all of a sudden shouted "What do you know about people? Your experience about life is very meagre but you claim as if you know all things about the world". Listening to the rebuke laden tone of her mother-in-law, the girl kept quiet but the senior lady went on shouting and condemning her *bahu* only on account of her not agreeing to what she had said. After a short time she started to pack up her things in her suitcase and said to her son, "I shall be going back to my home by the evening train." Listening to his mother's verdict, the boy was slightly disturbed and told her not to leave so soon as she was with them only for a couple of days. But she retorted, "I don't like to stay with the people who don't like to respect their elders." When the girl heard all that she went close to her mother-in-law and told her, "Dear Mother, I haven't said anything to you that you get so much disturbed and take a decision to go back. If still you feel that I have hurt your feelings, I seek your forgiveness. But don't go so early."

This sort of talk made her calm down and it looked that she would forget all what had happened a few minutes ago. Gradually, all started flowing smoothly. They ate well and watched some movie on the television. The start of the next day was quite smooth and after a while both, the boy & the girl went to their jobs. After they returned home from their work, the girl (*bahu*) started doing her routine cooking and preparing dinner for the family. The senior lady also helped her in the kitchen while the girl was cooking. But people who possess too much ego don't forget things so easily. They go on finding faults in different ways and pointing out certain other things relating different matters that may lead to involving in skirmishes and quarrels. The senior lady was also of that kind. She would not forget things so easily. When they started eating the dinner all of a sudden she reflected, "Well, food is quite good but there is more salt in the *dal* and less *jeera* in the curd. The *bahu* did not react at all though she did not like her comments. Salt in dal was put by her only.

When there was no reaction on the part of *bahu* the senior lady said something more that was further biting. "It looks that your mother did not give you enough training in cooking." Obviously the girl did not like that comment but did not utter a word just to avoid any skirmishes. That did not satisfy the lady. She suddenly started shouting, "Well, well, you now keep quiet and don't respond to what I have been saying." Perhaps this did not let the girl stay quiet for long. She, out of her frustration and dismay, abruptly said in a very low voice, "Oh, it is so difficult to stay here. If you talk then you are at fault, and when don't talk, you are still wrong." Hearing that low voiced comment, the senior lady's anger had no bounds. She started talking very loudly and condemning the girl repeatedly. She then asked her son, to send her away at once. The boy was greatly in distress and coming close to his mother he said to her respectfully, "Mother, she has not said anything to you that would be insulting or hurting. I request you just to forget all and live with us with affection and love you usually give us in the past." Well, all that did not satisfy the lady and she insisted that the *bahu* must be sent away at once or she might leave the house right then.

The boy was greatly distressed with such happenings. Anyhow, he tried to pacify the mother for time being in different ways so that everyone could sleep as it was already quite late in the night.

When they got up in the morning, the lady went on with the same old song which contained the wordings desiring the *bahu* to leave the house or she would quit at once. Out of frustration and agony, the boy had to ask his wife to quit for work a little early so that something could be sorted out between him and the mother. With tears in her eyes, the *bahu* got ready and left for work a little early than the scheduled time. When she came back from work, she learnt from her husband that the lady had left for her home which was in a different town and far away from their place. One needed at least 6 hours to reach there by an express bus. Both, the husband and the wife remained quiet for some time after meeting each other. Then the girl started her routine work of cooking and taking care of other important things needed at that time. They could not sleep that night until quite late, thinking about what had happened the previous day. Repeatedly, those thoughts visited their memory. Ultimately, the boy decided that she should go back to her mother's place for a couple of days for a change, so that he would be able to settle down with his mother. After coming to that decision, both went for a short sleep as much of the time had already gone in talking about the previous day's happenings.

Thus, ego distorts relationships so badly that people don't look back and think about others' happiness or peace. They only want to get satisfaction of their ego even though their own children are hurt or their lives get disturbed. Hurting back rarely satisfies one. Rather, it generates anger and the ego gets further stronger cradling a strong desire to take revenge and hurt as hard as possible. Let us contemplate on it a little more.

3

Hurting Back Rarely Satisfies

We have already said a little on 'hurting back hardly satisfies anyone. But more incidents are coming back to my memory in that context and I am reminded of a strange happening that took place around sixty years back when I was a student in a post-graduate college, completing my Master's Degree, in the capital town of my state, which lies around 400 miles away from my home town. As I started living there with different sorts of fellow hostlers, gradually, I learnt about other inmates who were also living in the same hostel. There were in all about eighty students residing in two stories of the hostel building. Fortunately, I got a bigger corner room at the ground floor. My roommate was from a different town but belonged to my own state and was fairly a good person with whom one could easily pull on.

Among these hostlers some of them were my classmates who were also completing the same master's course I was involved with. One of them, who did not live far away from my room, gradually became my fast friend. As the days passed on, we started enjoying our stay in the hostel and the loneliness, which makes one suffer initially when one leaves one's home first time, gradually started precipitating from our lives. Usually, we ate together, shared ideas about others and often studied in one room, either in mine or in his room until late in the night and go on drinking tea as many times as we desired. Life became much easy and we started dreaming for our progressive future. We often stayed in the hostel during short holidays from the college except at the occasions when there were holidays during *Holi* & *Deepawali* festivals. Once during *Holi* festival when my friend went home and stayed there a little longer. Finally, he came back and started attending classes.

When we met in the evening after coming back from the college, he asked me to visit his room just for a few minutes. As I entered his room, he closed the doors of his room and asked me to sit down for a while. Then he opened his closet, took out a small container and offered me the sweets that he had bought from his home, made by his mother. It was really a good and taste piece of sweet. As I liked it, the friend offered me one more piece of it and told me not to disclose the news of the sweets to anyone else in the hostel. Without taking it seriously, I said, "yes, I will not" and I left his room.

However, hostel life is a strange period of once life, when certain things are not taken seriously. I, therefore, did not consider my friend's advice to keep the news of the sweets secret. On my way back to my room from my friend's room, I happened to meet a common friend of ours. He was happy to see me coming from my friend's room and inquired how he was. I said he was fine and also disclosed the news of the sweets to him telling him that our friend had brought very good sweets from home. Listening to it, the other friend said that he must visit him as soon as possible lest all the sweets were finished by the friend who had brought them.

I did not realise by then that I should have not disclosed it at all to anyone, even to our common friends, that my friend had brought some sweets. The same day when I met my sweet bearer friend in the dining room, he did not talk to me and changed his seat to stay far away from me. Looking at him I felt surprised and went close to ask him to ask him why he did not like to sit by my side. Without responding to me, he went out of the dining room & did not come back for long though I went on waiting for him for a pretty long time. The next day, when we met in the college and entered the classroom, he changed the seat he often used to sit on without exchanging a word with me. I then concluded that my friend was very angry with me on certain account. So, after the class I approached him and asked him, "Kindly tell me what makes you so angry with me that you have stopped talking to me and even you don't like sit by me?"

Listening to that, the friend looked at me with stern eyes and said, "I told you not to disclose anybody that I had brought sweets from home, but you told everyone." In fact, I had not disclosed to anyone else than our common friend, considering that he would not even talk about the sweets to the friend who had brought them. Instead, the common friend disclosed about it to several hostel-mates whom he knew closely. Consequently, everyone of them gradually reached the sweet bearer friend and one by one all the pieces of sweets that he had brought for his own use, disappeared from his stock. Listening to all that I was a bit surprised and unhappy too. It was my mistake to trust that common friend and to disclose what I should have not. I apologised to him and said that I did not mean all that at all. But he was so angry, that he said to me with a disgusting and disappointing expression, "I don't want to keep any relations with you. In future you will never try to see me." Saying that he departed away from me. It is natural to strike back when you are hurt. The sweet bearer friend did the same to me and nothing was wrong on his part in taking that decision. But should he not accept my apologies and discuss the matter clearly before breaking with me. My continued apologies did not matter much to him. The only thing he wanted right at that time was to severe relations with me.

After being separated with a close friend just on a small issue, bothered me a lot. The sweet bearing friend too looked disturbed. Soon most people in the hostel gradually learnt all what had happened between us. Some really wondered that quite mature persons like me and the friend who broke with me, did not even give a second thought to the issue. For sometime we both became a laughing stock to the hostel inmates who sometimes passed unusual remarks when we passed by them. More than a month passed since the event of sweets took place. One day I learnt that my close friend, who had brought sweets, was terribly sick and was admitted to the hostel sickroom. It was confirmed by a doctor's regular visits to that room. I also confirmed on inquiring some inmates that my separated friend was sick and admitted in the sick room. The moment it was confirmed that it was my friend who was sick, I gradually became restless and desired to visit him to inquire how he was. But I was a little scared lest he should ask me to get out when I visit him. However, such a pathetic situation went on and on until one evening I decided to visit my sick friend.

It was around 7 p.m. when I went to see him. He was all alone in the sick room at that time. The moment he saw me entering the room he got up from the seat and ran to hug me. I too reciprocated the same. For a couple of minutes we went on hugging each other & tears ran through our eyes. I then asked him how he was and what caused his sickness. In a light mood I cracked, "Hope overeating of the sweets did not cause it?" The friend just laughed and narrated all that led to his sickness. I was so sorry to learn all that and asked him if I could do anything right then if he desired. The friend said that he did not need anything at that time but my presence made a great difference in our relationship. We started moving a little more strongly and promised never to be separated in life again.

It is true, hurting back never satisfies. Rather, it redoubles the hatred causing further separation, increasing ill-will, and accelerating enmity further. One can, therefore, decide what is right when some tense situation arises in one's relationship—whether one should hurt back or follow some other course which could help precipitating the dim situation.

Mental Reactions

In fact, it is all mind that reacts at difficult and different situations and makes one to move in the right or wrong direction. If one could control one's mind or is able to see distinctly what has been going on in it (as a result of reactions to a certain situation), one could amend oneself. But it does not happen that way. Often one reacts to any situation. Just for example, if one praises your make up or dressing style and tells you, "You are looking so smart today." You would naturally thank him/her and try secretly looking to your dress or may even go in front of a mirror to observe how smart you are looking. Thus, it is so natural to react on every kind of situation. However, some may react overtly a little more and others may not show their reaction but it certainly goes on inwardly.

At this juncture I recall an incidence which took place some twenty five years back in one of my B.Ed. final classes while I was teaching abroad. Generally, I would distribute the checked assignments to my students and ask them to go through my comments on them carefully. Then asked them let me know if they understood the meaning of the comments well. The intention was that next time they didn't repeat those mistakes again. When after distributing the assignment and giving the students sometime to go through them, I asked them whether all was clear to them. Most of them gradually reflected. "Yes sir, it is all clear," but one of the students stood up firmly on his seat and said to me loudly, "Sir, I don't agree what you have written on it." Listening to him I felt hurt and insulted. Consequently, my anger accelerated. I just asked him to bring the assignment to me. When he brought it to me I looked at it carefully once again, read my comments, which said, "Poor English." Since the student's English was poor, I wrote a strong remark on it about his way of expressing things as well as his faulty English. I was terribly annoyed at the student's reaction on my comments as what I had written was absolutely right as far as that assignment was concerned.

Instantly, I went through the assignment once again and discovered more mistakes in it. I crossed them also just in front of the student and told him in anger, "What do you say now?" The student replied submissively, "Sir, I still don't agree with you." Listening to his reply, I thought for a while and cut off my earlier remark. Instead I wrote on it, "Please improve your English." Looking at my changed remark, which was perhaps not derogatory or hurting, though intended for improvement, the boy became emotional and after paying me due respect, departed from me to take his seat. When I cut off my harsh remark, I realized that it was really hurting. In fact, I should have written a reformatory comment on the assignment rather than a biting one.

Therefore, if one feels guilty on any account, one is likely to react against it to cover up the guilt or mistake and could go on defending oneself in various ways. Very often it is the 'guilt feeling' caused on any account that often creates problems and makes one react to do something against it. We will talk about it a little later in this chapter, but right now I happen to recall a small incidence that took place around fifty years back when I was a student of Master's Course in Education.

One of our senior professors, a lady, who was well-spoken and quite good looking, would always come to the college well-dressed, walked in a stylish manner and often entered the classroom humming some Hindi song. She loved music and played on harmonium very well. As a course requirement, just after a couple of weeks when the first semester had started, she asked us to complete some assignment and return that to her in a week's time after completing it carefully.

On the particular date when the assignment was due to be handed over to her, we all reached the class on time. When she arrived in the class and settled down in her chair, she asked us to bring the assignment. After a minute I got up from my seat and tried to hand over my assignment to her respectfully. She thanked me to complete it on time but instead of receiving it, she asked me to read it before the class. As asked by her, I started reading it carefully. Hardly I had started reading it for a couple of minutes, that she shouted loudly, "Is it the right material that you have chosen for the assignment? It looks you did not work properly on it." I kept quiet for a minute and before I would say something, one of my classmates told her politely, "Madam, he had been working on it very hard for the last one week." Listening to my classmate's commending comments, she looked at me with unfriendly eyes and told me to read it again. By then I had lost my patience and was extremely angry on account of her unfriendly and unkind treatment. In fact, I had worked very hard on it. Besides, I had also consulted a couple of senior lecturers during my preparation. Listening to her bossy command, I kept quiet and did not read it. She again shouted loudly, "Read it again." But instead of reading it, I just walked out of the class, uttering something slowly but unpleasant. In rage I said to her, "I thought it was a Master's Class of Education, but instead it looks to be a class in a police college."

It was enough to hurt the professor, who considered herself to be special and very important in the college. Certainly it was also not right on my part to behave like that. I did not act prudently by hurting my egoist professor who would never accept such a behaviour from her own students. I reckon, I reacted as her remark about my assignment was not appropriate. She should have also not talked to me in that harsh tone which was hurting as well as meant to calculate me as a shirker from work. Whatever the case was, my on ego drove me to move out of the class and to say something quite unpleasant. One can imagine the remaining story of my career during my Master's class in Education. Yes, I passed the examination by obtaining quite good marks but as my professor was not happy with me, I did not get very good marks in all the papers she was in charge. What better example there would be relating, 'If you are hurt, it is natural to hurt back, but hurting back never satisfies' One goes on hurting others, creating more problems for oneself.

I like to relate something more about our lady professor, whom I tried to hurt as she showed her disbelief in me when I submitted the assignment. There is another story related to the same professor and the same assignments. It took place during the same time when the assignment was given to all of us. One of the students in our class, who too had to complete the assignment at the same time (when we all had to do it), could not complete it on time as his wife was ill and his children were small. He was one of the close friends of mine. When he completed the assignment almost after a week from the given date, he came to me to inquire about the professor's place of residence. She lived very near our hostel and I knew the place very well. The friend told me that his assignment was ready and he needed to submit it to her. I told my friend that the time to submit it had gone and she might not accept it. But he insisted that he would like to submit it to her right at that time as it was a Sunday and she could easily be available at her house. He had already told me the reasons for its late submission.

Reluctantly I accompanied my friend. When we reached her quarters, we rang the bell. Listening to the bell she appeared at the door and asked "What has brought you both to my door at that hour?" My friend told her respectfully that as his wife was indisposed, he was unable to submit the assignment on time. Listening to my friend's humble appeal, she extended her hand to receive it. But as soon as she took it in her hand, she threw it far away instantly. Not only that, she also started scolding my friend of being lazy and not working according to the rules she had prescribed. We stood there in silence for sometime, but the friend, after sometime, slowly tracked towards his assignment which had fallen far in the professor's lawn. He collected it carefully, dusted it, slowing tracked back near her and tried to resubmit it politely. This time, though she collected it, but uttered something unpleasant. Watching and listening to all that, my blood started boiling, but as my friend behaved like a very humble person, he was able to submit the assignment to the unpleasant professor.

The result was good as the next day she talked good of my friend. She praised him in the class, though she also said that the assignment was submitted late, probably due his wife's illness. Considering all that, I finally concluded that it was always good not to react when one's circumstances were uneven. One should always act judiciously and in a positive way in all the circumstances even when situations of that nature arise in one's life. It will not only diffuse the odd situations, but also shun down the ill-wills that are caused due to reacting back unpleasantly.

4

Retaliation Gives, at Best, Momentary Respite: It does not Lessen the Sting

Retaliation may give someone momentary relief but it does not lessen the sting, the cause of hurting. We have already given some examples of that nature. How the lady professor reacted when two of us behaved in different ways! I acted against the circumstances, but the friend did not show any adverse reaction, though within he too was very unhappy. The truth is that none of us, me and my friend, were initially at fault. There could be several examples of that kind and can be quoted even from ordinary circumstances of one's life.

Just for example, when we travel in trains (especially in India) and if any senior person (in age) does not get his desired berth (a lower berth) in the reserved compartment, he might approach someone in the same compartment who is comparatively young and request him to go to a higher berth situated around four feet above his own. Quite often people agree to exchange berths but there may be some who would refuse to do. When such a situation arises, it may quite often depend on the mood of the person and the way the approach is made to the person whose berth is situated downwards. Often the approached persons agrees but sometimes, either due to some real reasons or fake reasons, one may not agree and refuse to shift from his own berth. More depends the way someone is approached. Thus, it is the way one reacts to a situation, and usually gets the results accordingly.

I remember how my two teachers in high school, on account of their behaviour in the class, were received by their students. One was respected and the other was disliked. The one, who was respected, was awarded with their love and complete obedience. The other, whom they did not like, was not internally respected and despised. The kind and caring one, was highly reverend. The other one always brought a small stick in his hand (some seventy years back from 2016) & as soon as he entered the class, would thresh it on the students' desks. At times he would hit it at their backs. It was never liked by the students. Therefore, it is one's own behaviour, the way one acts in favour or against someone or circumstances, that usually becomes responsible for the good or bad results. Thus, retaliation may bring respite for someone who retaliates, but it never makes him/her happy ultimately.

I have yet another example of retaliation which brought disaster in one's family and never made the retaliating person happy. It is a real incidence about an Indian origin boy, who studied in US after completing his initial degree in India. When he came to US for further studies, he worked very hard and completed his postgraduation in Engineering with distinguished position in the university. Consequently, some American companies offered him good openings. After taking over a job in one of the promising companies in US, he started living there smoothly. Once or twice his parents also visited him in two years duration. The boy, after fairly settling down in the job, started going to the clubs and 'working-out places' (usually called jims). It was during his visits to the jims, that he happened to meet an American girl who was working there as a temporary instructor. As her educational background was quite meagre, she could not find a better job than that. Both, the boy and the girl started visiting each other frequently and the girl usually would like to stay with the boy after her day's work when he too would come back from his work-place.

In India several families came to see the boy's parents with a suitable match for their son, offering their daughters in marriage. All the prospective girls possessed good education and some of them were also fruitfully employed in different towns in India. During the period when girls' parents were approaching the boy's father for marriage, the boy also happened to come to India to see his parents. One fine morning the father told his son that it was time for him to get married. He also disclosed to him that several parents had already approached him with quite suitable matches. As the boy was already having the America girl's company in US, he politely refused his parents for any such alliance. He said that he still had not made up his mind about it. So, there was no hurry for his marriage. In the mean time when he reached back US he married that American girl and informed his parents about it. The parents were not happy to get the news but as they wanted the son to stay happy in life, they reluctantly accepted the news.

Now, the real story begins. After staying with her Indian husband for almost ten years and having three children from him, one day the girl, who was fully grown up as a lady, told him that she wanted to divorce him. It was a great shock and surprise to him as he took great care of her and children. He had also helped her to get further education after the marriage and helped her to get in to a good job. He always cared for the family and spend his most of the income as per his wife's needs and demands. But the lady believed in spending most of her husband's income in useless purchases and buying toys and several other articles which were not really needed in a house even in America. She also started visiting ladies' clubs and spending lot of money on cards and would often stayed quite late in the night in the clubs. If her husband asked her not to spend money uselessly, she would turn a deaf ear to that and go on spending more instead, and would tell him to keep quiet. She often told him that she would do only what she liked.

Now, constant problems of different nature erupted everyday. Some were relating children and some about finances. It was an act of retaliation on her part as her husband would ask her not to waste money and help children in different ways. Instead, she acted differently. She would incite children to ask for different things so that more money could be spent. All that led to regular skirmishes and there was no peace in the house. When all that was going on one fine morning she told him firmly that she was going to stay away from him. That simply meant a divorce. Nothing could be done now except that he had to abide by it and pay her whatever was due according to the rules prevalent in the US. She has been living now all alone as children are usually with the father. She retaliated for her own enjoyment but she was finally paid as the God's rules are final and firm. To cut the story short, I would like to come to the main point that, '**Retaliation may *give a momentary respite but does not lessen the sting*.**

The Guilt Feeling

I have often observed that guilt feelings usually lead to reactions and retaliation in different ways. If someone drives his/her car with more than the permitted speed and if caught by the police, one may usually say that being in a great hurry due to certain problem, one was driving fast. In certain countries, where (even by 2016 in India) no speed limit is indicated on the road or prescribed by the road authorities, quite often youngsters like to experiment on the road by driving very fast without caring for their own and others' lives. When caught by the police, the usual pretense given by them to the police is, 'my mother or father or someone very close to him, has been hospitalized or taken ill all of a sudden, etc. So, I am running fast.' Likewise, when someone is caught telling lies, one is likely to react in a certain way which could simply meant to hide the lies. Some people often don't respond to their phone calls. When they are caught telling lies, they usually say "I did not hear the ring, or I was in the bathroom or I forgot my phone at home while I went to the market." All that could be true also, but only with those people who don't tell lies and so they don't need to defend themselves. They would usually tell the reasons of not picking up the phone.

At times, we also call it ***defense mechanism*** to react against a situation just to protect ourselves or to divert others' attention from us. If someone is caught doing something wrong, he/she might say, 'he was doing it just for this or that reason.' If the master of the house tells everyone in the house not to switch on the television until some particular time as he does not want to divert the attention of children from their studies, It happens so that often others who want to switch on to television, don't obey him. The guest or the servant working in that home ignores the master's advice and switches on the television. If caught, then often he/she might say, 'I was just checking whether the power was there or not. Or some other kind of pretense could be given by the defaulter. However, what pretense the Kauravs would give in unveiling Dropadi among all her relatives and other people. It was their own prejudices against their own cousins, the Pandavas. So, one needs to be very careful in reacting to an uneven situation and requires to restrain, need to think twice before acting or taking revenge or hurting others, for the consequences of such an action will surely be detrimental.

Thus, taking revenge against someone when hurt or insulted, is quite natural and there are always ways to lessen the sting as it constantly goes on causing problems. What could be those ways, need to be thought about carefully. If one acts thoughtfully and carefully at the occasion when hurt, bad consequences could easily be averted, many odd situations could be prevented. To my mind there are some ways which if followed properly, can help in averting a bad situation easily. Let us explore some of them.

Freedom of Mind

One such way has been suggested by the great philosopher and thinker Jiddu Krishnamurti, a South Indian, who showed great interest in seeking salvation from most of man's mental disturbances by constantly pushing out every kind of thought from mind and keep it free from them. He calls it '***thoughtless state of mind***' in which one just stops thinking anything and keeps the mind vacant from any thoughts. One can also call it '***freedom of mind***'. Krishnamurti holds that for such a state of mind one does not need to practice it. It can be done easily.

Though it looks easier to think about such a state of mind, in fact it is not so easy. When one tries to empty one's mind from thoughts, they go on coming into the mind and thus, one restarts thinking something inadvertently. However, Krishnamurti holds it quite differently. He reckons that no practice is needed for such a state of mind. It is just a way of keeping one's mind in that state. Perhaps, it would have been easy for Jidddu Krishnamurti to hold his mind free from any kind of thoughts, but it is not so easy for a common person who is not wonted to practice like that. Krishnamurti also strongly thought that no practice was needed for emptying one's mind from thoughts. One needed to sit or stay in a meditative posture or position, and go on removing thoughts from one's mind as they start appearing in it. I reckon, for such a state of mind, one has to go on and on constantly averting the coming thoughts out of one's mind. In the beginning, it may look quite difficult, but gradually as one goes on trying to remove one's thoughts out of the mind one by one, one can do so and the state of tranquility could be achieved.

When one comes to such a state of serenity in mind, it becomes easy for him/her to see clearly. As the dense forest of worries and hurts that has been puzzling the mind for so long, is pushed aside, one can easily discover the cause of being hurt and may not try returning it back. Thus, the idea of hurting back could gradually be subsided and peace may be installed. It may take either the form of forgiveness or if one does not forgive right at that time, one may postpone the idea of hurting back immediately. He/she may even think to give another chance to the person who inflicted any pain to you. Whatever be the case, one may not immediately think of hurting back if one tries strongly to keep one's mind free from such things.

Controlling the Mind

In order to keep one's mind free from erratic thoughts, it is absolutely necessary to keep it controlled so that no ill thoughts try entering into it. Not only when one is hurt by someone that one needs to keep control on the mind, it is always necessary to keep it controlled under every circumstance and situation. Wise people always keep their minds free from every kind of ill thoughts by constantly controlling and pushing away them out. The revered Buddha has rightly expressed the state of a wise person in the Dhammapada:

By rousing himself, by earnestness, by restraint and control, the wise man may make for himself an island which no flood can overwhelm.

The problem arises only when one does not think properly and react as soon as wrong thoughts invade the mind. It is also quite natural to react when one feels insulted or gets hurt through words or physically. Thus, the chain of getting hurt and hurting back goes on and on. Just for example, if someone abuses you, you may instantly react and start saying bad things to him. Then the chain of abuses goes on continuously which may ultimately result in fighting orally or physically and consequently wounding both or anyone of them. Therefore, controlling one's mind is not only needed at the occasions when someone hurts you, it is also greatly beneficial in many respects.

At this juncture, I remember a real story of a man who was abused right in front of his house in my presence as I was going to school at that time. I was just a high school student then. The man who was abusing, was the next door neighbour of the person whom he was hurling filthy abuses. When the abusing man exhausted all his abuses, the one to whom the abuses were given, came closer to the abuser and told him politely: "Whatever you have given me just now, I return all that to you as it is." We all, who had stopped to witness the odd scenario, started laughing at the situation. When we looked at the face of the abuser, we all were surprised. With tight lips he looked confusedly at his prey. He had nothing left to say or to do and looked totally confused. In fact, he did not know what to say after that. He then slowly went back to his house. But before he left he uttered sluggishly, "What a strange fellow!"

Yet, there is another small story of two mendicants, who, before staring their journey to a certain place, pledged that would not touch any woman in their lives as that was against the rules of their saintly practices. One day while they were about to cross a river, they saw a woman who too was waiting to go to the other side of the river. There was no boat available at the river at that time. One of the mendicants, who was comparatively kinder and wise as well, asked her whether she wanted to go the other side of the river. The woman nodded positively. Then the mendicant beckoned her to come closer and tied her behind his back. He then gradually swam across the river along with the woman. When he came to the other side of the river, he untied her, left her there and continued his journey with his companion.

They had hardly gone for some distance after crossing the river that the other companion stopped and told his fellow mendicant, "You have broken the rules of the saintly practices. Why did you carried the woman on your back when we had pledged not to touch any women?" The mendicant who had carried the woman on his back just smiled to hear him and said politely, "I have left the woman far behind on the bank of the river, but you are still carrying her in your mind."

Therefore, wrong and unkind thoughts which identify others' weaknesses, often go on invading our minds and keeping us awake whole night. Can we just try to shun them down and keep our minds empty from such sick and mean thoughts which only give us turmoil, hatred and dislike for others? If we can think better and wisely, we may live far away from those thoughts and stay better among our own people, distributing love and happiness and making them all blissful.

The Art of Letting Go

At this juncture, I wish to quote from Buddha's Book on meditations, named **"Buddha Meditations: The Art of Letting Go."** It says, "We want more control in our lives, and we often act as if it's all about controlling the people and things around us. Too often we focus on the others we want to direct and to affect what that they decide, think of us, vote, buy, and do." All this surely leads to different sorts of problems for us. He further comments: "Imagine if instead we practice to know, to develop, and to control our own minds—to recognise, and let go of, chatter about petty worries, problems that haven't happened yet, gossips, replayed hurts, plots for revenge or gain, yearning for things we don't have. Imagine just feeling in love with being part of the whole glorious splendour of life." If we can do so, the meaning of our life will surely change positively.

When Julius Ceaser was stabbed by his very close ally, Brutus, he was shocked. Brutus did it not to please his own friends and allies but for his benefit, to capture power and rule on Greek. Just before stabbing Ceaser, he criticised him and accused him that he might misuse the power that he had achieved by his recent victories. He never thought a second time that Julius's own close faithful ally Antonio, who was also a strong warrior, might kill Brutus and all the people who had been involved in killing Ceaser. If Brutus had not allied other people in killing Ceaser, he would have not been killed and the history of Rome would have been quite different.

Thus, at times 'the art of letting go' is of great importance, for that helps to avert some dreadful situation of which we normally don't think about earlier. But we normally don't do so and without discerning our own emotional patterns, greed and self-interests, go on acting unwisely. Buddha comments: "Imagine if we could discern our own emotional patterns and ways of thinking, recognising the negative habits and impulses, and say goodbye to them in a way that didn't cause harm. Imagine of loving kindness replaced gossip, and joy replaced judgment."

But can it be done so easily and the on-coming bad situation could be averted smoothly? Yes, Buddha suggests some ways which are surely effective to push away us from the ill-feelings. Besides 'letting go things', he also suggests performing meditation. For centuries, Buddhists have used meditation as the transformation way to replace the unwholesome with the wholesome. Lisa TE Sonne, the writer of Buddha Meditation, who had deep understanding of Buddhist thoughts and philosophy, reflects:

"Sometimes, our day's emotions and thoughts fill us with anger, worries, self-doubts, and other half-chewed garbage. We may think we are 'letting go' of all that when we reach for drink or turn on the television, but the next day those negative feelings will still be there. Meditation can help us 'let go' of those unneeded thoughts." Thus, regular meditation can be helpful to a large extent to redeem our ills and diffuse the ill feelings that cause anger, frustration and lead us to retaliation against others.

In no way retaliation is appropriate, neither for the person's own-self who cradles it in his/her own thoughts as such thoughts go on disturbing the person constantly, nor it is good to retaliate to others as it would bring disaster in relationships and go on keeping one constantly unhappy and disturbed. Therefore, the right way would be to ignore such thoughts which give birth to retaliation. But it is not easy to do so. For cultivating good state of mind, one must train the mind in some way. One of such ways which has been considered good for so long by the Buddhists, is practicing meditation. Let us reflect little more on that aspect.

The Value of Meditation

The value of meditation is sometimes correlated by gardening says Lisa TE Sonne. "Meditation can help plant and cultivate the good seeds. It probably won't kill the bad seeds (desire, greed, jealousy, anger, regret...).They continue to exist, but they may stay dormant, and not do harm, if not watered and fed with negative thoughts. If we pull out the weeds by their roots, we can better see the flowers and give them more room to grow." (p.37)

Sonne continues reflecting on the advantages of meditation which can certainly help shunning down our adverse and negative thoughts. He states that when we meditate we start possessing a still mind. When the mind becomes still, it becomes like a tranquil surface of an unperturbed lake or clean mirror, reflections appear that were not visible earlier. One can see birds and clouds come and go and also see oneself more clearly. If one goes on doing meditation, one may gradually learn to tame the inner animal and manage the mind. (p.38)

Continuing the importance and value of meditation, Sonne reflects further. Meditation can help us reset our well-being. If we are not spending our energy by uselessly running away from things, or running towards the things that usually attract us and try stay still, it will make things come to us from within. That will make everything clear, helping us to understand the meanings of things not clear to us earlier, and we may be saved from retaliating against others when they hurt us, saving us from several problems that would follow after we retaliate.

Whenever I was in a pensive mood on account of recalling some hurt inflicted by someone, especially by one who was my own, I discovered an easy way to keep myself away from those burning thoughts. I often left my room or place and went for a walk. More than that I visited one of my close and trustworthy friends in whom I relied a lot and could unlock my worries and share my injured feelings with him. With a changed climate and friend's warm welcome, much of the worry and hurt feelings were gradually toned down giving me a lot of peace and comfort. That made me take a comfortable slumber, and when I got up next day, it looked that all was afresh and new.

Thus, one can find several ways to cut off the biting feelings caused on account of someone's unkind acts, can stay cool and lead a productive life which provides satisfaction, happiness and comfort. But regular yogic exercises are always beneficial and help us keeping healthy as well as serene which are the ways to live long as well as to live in peace.

❑❑❑

5

Until We Forgive, We Stay Locked in Our Pain: Without Forgiving We Remain Tethered to the Feeling or the Person

Until we forgive the person who has inflicted pain and hurt our feelings, we remain bound to the hurt feelings and stay tethered to them. As the pain continues, we remain locked out of the possibility of experiencing any healing and freedom, locked out of the possibility of being at peace and happiness. Once again at this juncture I recall the story of my friend who had brought some sweets from home and told me not to disclose the news of sweets to anyone in the college hostel where we were living at that time. It has been narrated in some previous chapter. As I disclosed that to someone, the friend got annoyed and we both separated for couple of months. We did not like to see each other at all even if we studied in the same class in the college. But all subsided when my friend fell ill and was admitted in the hostel sick room. We both missed each other at that time forgetting the ill feelings. Finally, when I visited him in the sick room, we embraced each other and forgot all the ill feelings. But until we totally forgot our ill feelings, we did not like even to look at each other.

Without forgiveness, we go on remembering the person who has inflicted injury to us. 'We go on remembering the incidences and are bound with chains of bitterness, tied together, trapped. Until we can forgive the person who has harmed us, that person will hold the key of our happiness', reflects Archbishop Tutu.

At this juncture, once again I am reminded again of the incidence when a son started thrashing his father as the father used to beat his mother when the son was young. The son kept the hurt feelings within for years. When he grew young and got a chance to project his hurt feeling, he projected them by assaulting his father. Therefore, without cradling forgiveness in one's heart, it becomes very difficult to forgive the person who has inflicted any injury to you. Though possessing a demeanor like that of the Buddha (Siddarth) even when he was very young, is very difficult, we can still try for that.

Once, when Siddarth's (Gautama's) cousin Devadutta, tried to hurt him as he wanted to take back the bird he had hunted by his arrow, Siddarth refused to give it to him. Instead, he continued tending the bird to protect its life. Devadutta was very angry with Siddarth and was ready to fight to take the bird back from him. But Gautama did not give him the bird. Though keeping patience at the occasions when someone wants to hurt you or desires to inflict pain to you is extremely difficult, and we as human beings easily react on such occasions, but Siddarth did not react. He did not listen to Devadutta and continued tending the wounded bird. Thus, if one can exert patience for sometime, peace will gradually prevail and one can avert lots of problems that usually follow on account of reacting against the hurt feelings. Let us clarify it further by narrating a legendry tale.

Practice of Patience

It is imperative that persons who possess aggressive demeanor, need to contain themselves by cradling patience within as without that they are likely to be aggressive. A beautiful example of that sort is found in the legends relating the tales of Buddha. "An ascetic named Ksantivadin, who was subjected to torture by a wrongly wrathful king, but who nonetheless endured all his suffering without so much as a single thought of ill-will towards his tormentor." (John S Strong: p.30)

I reckon, most problems arise in life when we don't keep patience. We go on fighting on small matters and start denouncing each other. It ultimately leads to bigger problems. Just for example if in a house there is only one toilet or bath and several persons want to share it just at one time, trouble is likely to erupt. If the persons living there are wise and can keep patience, things would go smoothly without any problems. But instead if all want to use the bathroom just at the same time, skirmishes are likely to break up between the people who reside there. Let me remind a few real tales of some humans who by their kind and forgiving demeanor, and possessing colossal patience, are known as the embodiments of kindness and epitome of divinity.

Jesus Christ

Can one compare with the real story of Jesus Christ, who when conducted to the gallows for hanging him on the crossed board, seeks God's forgiveness for all those people who inflicted severe injuries on his body and went on jeering at him throughout the way until he was crucified. Different kinds of people followed him when he was conducted by the Roman armed personnel to the cross-boards where he was to be nailed. In between, whenever he tried to stop even for a moment to bear his physical and internal pain, he prayed to the Lord. But the moment he stopped, the Romans conducting him would whip him severely. As the whips fell on his bare and lean body, he would often bent down with pain and try to endure it and prayed to the Lord to give him more courage to bear all that pain. Besides, he also implored Him to 'forgive all those who were inflicting pain and injury.'

I have never come across in the history of mankind such a story of compassion and extreme kindness that those who are tormenting you physically, should be forgiven by the one who is being tortured. Not only that, he is also pleading for God's forgiveness for them as they are totally ignorant of doing what they are doing. What an expression of compassion and extreme kindness. Yes, we cannot reach the height that Lord Christ reached by his constant prayers and extreme compassion for the mankind, especially for all those who are weak and poor. But at least we can keep patience when we encounter problems and suffer from injuries inflicted by others.

The Buddha

There is another real story of a human being who though came to know that he had been poised by someone of his own, but he forgave him for he too was extremely compassionate and benevolence incarnate. It is the story of Gautama Buddha who at the age of eighty, after travelling a long distance during that day, stopped at some place to take night's rest. It was supper time when one of his old disciples Kunda, who belonged to the place where the Buddha had stopped for that night, brought him some food to eat. The Buddha ate it pleasingly but as soon as he finished eating, he fell sick. The disciple had brought that food for him with great affection but he did not know that the food was contaminated and poisonous. If he knew it he would have never offered that food to his reverend teacher.

As soon as the Buddha ate it, he felt pain in his stomach and instantly discovered that the food was contaminated. But it was too late by then and finally he succumbed to death that night. But before dying, he called Ananda, one his very affectionate and close disciples, who was also taking care of him all the time. He told Ananda, 'Please tell Kunda that I don't have any ill-will against him for I know that Kunda would have never given me that food deliberately if he knew that it was poisonous.' This true story is almost equivalent to that of the Christ. Both Christ and Buddha knew before their death who were their killers but they forgave them just before their death. Christ even prayed to God to forgive all those who were involved in torturing him before his death.

Yes, it is true that we cannot reach the height of Christ or Buddha as far as their compassionate demeanor is concerned but we can at least learn not to react immediately when we are hurt by someone and keep patience for sometime so that either we forget the incidence and forgive the person who has inflicted any pain. It looks easier to write but not really so easy but at least we can try it. And even if we try postponing our attitude of reacting immediately, I am confident, things will improve to a large extent. I have experimented about it. As we all are likely to meet such situations everyday in our lives, we can try to postponing reacting immediately against them by keeping patience.

Socrates

Though the story of Socrates of Greece is not quite equivalent to that of the Christ and Buddha's, in some way it has some sort of similarity as he too was killed by his own countrymen because he loved truth and would not deviate from it even if his life was in danger. Around 470 B.C. in Greece, Socrates started teaching people to practice truth and lead a life of righteousness which did not recommend worshiping so many gods and goddesses. Socrates strongly believed that there was only one God and only He should be worshiped instead. During those days people in Greece held the beliefs which contained worshiping of several gods and deities and celebrating ceremonies which have no relationship to lead a straight life.

Socrates considered all such ceremonies and blind beliefs useless as they would never help human beings to lead a pure and religious life. With his own strong belief in righteousness he regularly taught his disciples accordingly. Socrates always emphasised the importance of the mind over the relative unimportance of the human body. This doctrine inspired Plato's philosophy of dividing reality into two separate realms, the world of the senses and the world of ideas, declaring that the latter was the only important one. Socrates believed that philosophy should achieve practical results for the greater well-being of society. He attempted to establish an ethical system based on human reason rather than theological doctrine. He pointed out that human choice was motivated by the desire for happiness. Ultimate wisdom comes from knowing oneself. The more a person knows, the greater is his or her ability to reason and to make choices that will bring true happiness.

When Greek authorities came to know about Socrates's activities, they ordered him not to propagate against the Greek systems as that would mean treason and a revolt against the Greek way of leading common life. But Socrates did not stop talking about his beliefs he considered sane and related to the truth. So, he was arrested. He was kept in jail for sometime to change. But he refused to change. Consequently, he was offered to drink hemlock (poison) to embrace death. All that took place around 399 B.C.

Considering Socrates's story important and relating to our theme of "Forgiveness", I would emphasise that Socrates pointed out that human choice was more motivated by the desire for happiness. But ultimate wisdom comes only from knowing oneself. The more a person knows his own self, the greater becomes the ability to reason and make choices that bring true happiness. The ***more a person understands the reason of someone's reactions*** against anyone, the better he/she understands the cause of reacting against others. Reactions usually go on and on due to self-interests and when one does not get any advantage from the persons(s) involved with that particular situation, problem arises.

Just for example, if you refuse to give certain things your children asking you to provide them, they are likely to react against you.

Probably, some children may not react overtly to your denial of things to them, but some may certainly show it overtly and push you to the realm of reacting against them. Such a reaction is likely to throw you to the region of disappointment and may involve you to a chain of reactions which may go on for quite a long time providing you lot of mental turmoil. Therefore, one must learn specifically that without forgiving the hurts made against us, we would remain tethered to the feeling or the person.

At this juncture, I am reminded of Gandhi's story which unfolds how he kept patience even in the presence of his own killer and did not react at all when someone shot at him while he was praying at an open praying ground in Delhi when scores of people were attending that prayer session.

Gandhi

Quite similar to the above stories, is also another real life story of Mahatma Gandhi who sacrificed his life for the good of the country advising people of different communities to live together friendly like brothers. When India became Independent, he would often go to a particular prayer ground in Delhi and offered prayers to God among lots of people who often came to listen to him. Since he was highly reverend by most of the people in India except a very few, who did not like his sermons relating the unity of different communities living in India, they condemned such sermons and planned to kill him. Consequently, one of evening when he had just finished his prayers and a short sermon, someone just came before him and pulled his pistol to kill him. Gandhi, when looked at his killer, greeted him with folded hands as traditionally Indians often do. As soon as he folded his hands, the shooter shot him several times and tried to run away. But he was caught and later on hanged.

I have narrated this story just to stress the point that it is not necessary that you must react to every situation adversely and start hurting others. If Gandhi Ji wanted, he would bow down to escape shots from the pistol or would start shouting for help of others to save his life. Instead, he saluted the killer by folding his hands and took all the shots into his body. Perhaps, it a kind of different example, but it does convey that if we strongly desire, we would not react to any odd situation and avoid problems that usually follow when one is hurt and react against that hurt.

Once again I am reminded of the situation which I narrated in some earlier chapter about my friend, going to the professor to hand over his assignment that he could not complete on time. If I really understood the professor's nature and her demeanor as my friend did, I too would have not reacted to her harsh behaviour in the class when she asked me to read out the assignment. But my friend, who was not able to submit his assignment on time, not only tried to understand her nature, he also did not react when his assignment was thrown away by her. Instead, he kept cool and silently tracked to collect his thrown away assignment. Then he humbly handed over it to her once again. Finally, she took it back as she did not know what to do then. It was also very much out of the point to throw it once again.

It is, therefore, very much important to avoid reacting to any kind of odd situation. But all such learning would primarily depend on one's ***practice of keeping cool when odd situation arises.*** So, let us try to make a rule in our life that we would ***always cultivate patience*** and never abandon it any moment, especially when surrounded by difficult or odd circumstances.

Mental Confusion

I strongly feel, at this juncture, to talk about 'mental confusion' which often adds to reactions and leads one to react to odd circumstances. In one of my books "***Happiness Is Divine***" written around 2010, I have created a chapter on 'Remove the Mind-

Fetters' so that you can live happily. I would like to project some important ideas from there as that relates to our current theme of "Forgiveness'.

People often react to situations as their mental state is not normal on account of their erroneous thinking. "There are people who always feel that there is something wrong with them and everyday when they get up, they live in hang-ups, doubts and confusion and with a kind of feeling that makes them believe that something is going to happen with them. The fact is that these mind-shackles have no real existence, yet they appear real to some people. I reckon that it is rather impractical to attain even a small fragment of happiness without removing these mind-fetters. State of happiness is the state of mind in which it is completely free from any kind of strain, hang-ups or impediments. It is therefore imperative to remove these hang-ups or roadblocks from the minds to get finished happiness."…..

"Though these mind-barriers have no real existence, they bother us tremendously. Therefore, they must be dealt with strongly if we wish to live happily. Dr. Norman Vincent Peale believes that there are four majour mental hang-ups. Nearly either one or the other is always casting its shadow over the problem-ridden people. The four mental hang-ups that Dr. Peale indicates are ***self-doubt, resentment, guilt*** and ***worry***." (pp. 6-7) I include two more to that list of Dr. Peale. It is ***jealousy*** and ***ego***. People often harbour some kind of jealousy against others without any reasons. They go on keeping ego & envy even without the knowledge of the others against whom they keep these odd feelings. These are such kinds of mental hang-ups that always keep people alert in thinking against others. All that become great barriers to human happiness.

Let us discuss each one of them separately for each one of them has some sort of relationship with our main theme "Forgiveness".

When people are not able to forget and forgive, they are likely to hurt others.

Quite often people suffer with the feeling that they have problems which they cannot solve. But they will never think that they are quite capable to solve their own problems of several kinds if they really desire so. A great thinker named Emerson once reflected, "A man is what he thinks about all day long." Therefore, if one thinks about success, he would work hard to create circumstances which may lead him/her to success. But if one contemplates of failure, it is he/she alone who sets the stage for that. I remember at this stage how one of my friends mostly believed that he was unwell. On my inquiry about what kind of illness he possessed, he told me that he suffered from many kinds of problems. That included high blood pressure, fever, indigestion etc. When I asked him whether he consulted a doctor, he replied that he did not, but he was sure of all those kinds of illness he possessed.

With my continued insistence, I made him agree to go to a doctor. Finally, he agreed to visit a doctor we both knew closely. The doctor declared that except indigestion, he did not have any of those sorts of illness he was believing to possess. Thus, it is often ***self-doubt*** that make people afraid to stand up to their own problems. But if one stands up to his/her own problems, very often those difficulties would not stand up. When people are not able to stand against their own problems, they are likely to create problems for others too and go on hurting them just to cover up their own inadequacies.

I narrate one very important and true story of a human being who gradually controlled his inadequacy completely as he had confidence in himself and was determined to control that weakness by hard labour and constant practice. When I read Winston Churchill's life story, I was greatly amazed and inspired. Churchill used to stammer when he was holding the War-office in England.

But he was self-confident to defeat his speech impediment. So, he constantly gave dictations to his secretary. With colossal confidence and constantly giving dictations to his secretary, he was able to win over his stammering. In fact, it is the self-confidence to a great extent which can help the mind ridden people from indulging with the feeling that 'something is wrong with them'. Even if there is something wrong, they can gradually defeat that. It will save them in two ways. One—they will stay free from self-doubt and two—they may not think to inflict pain on others by not hurting them.

By learning the life stories of such people like Churchill or Mahatma Gandhi who never yielded to their odd circumstances, one can defeat one's self-doubting attitudes. There is other way too to forget one's doubts and divert attention from such nasty thoughts. Just recall examples from religion—either from the Bible or the *Gita*. A very strong call to courage can be found in Joshua 1:9. It unfolds,

"Be strong and of a good courage; be not afraid, neither be thou dismayed: for the
Lord they God is with thee whithersoever thou goest."

Or if you can go through the *Bhagwat Gita*, you will find there too such ideas being lucidly implicit. When Arjun looks at his own kinsmen stationed in their own ranks, gathered to fight against him, he becomes doleful and confused. In that state of confusion he speaks to Sri Krishna:

"Seeing O Krishna, these my kinsmen gathered here eager to fight,
my limbs fail me and my mouth is perched up. I shiver all over,
and my hair stands on end..." Gita Ch. I Verse 28-29.

Hearing all that and realising that Arjun was totally confused, Sri Krishna tell him:

"In such a crisis, whence comes upon thee, O Arjuna,
this dejection, un-Arya-like, disgraceful, and contrary

to the attainment of heaven. Yield not to unmanliness, O son of Pritha! Ill doth it become thee. Cast off this mean faint-heartedness and arise, O scorcher of thine enemies." Gita Chapter II Verse 2-3.

When we become weak on account of any reason, there cannot be better examples anywhere than we discover in religion. By reading such messages from the holy books and by constantly keeping our thoughts on them, we can gradually cast away the doubting attitude. I implore the people who usually get weakened on account of confusion, to recall such examples from religious books and bring them to the forefront of their minds. If one can do so, one would surely sink those problems deep down into certain region of one's mind and become free from the confused state of mind. ***Changing patterns of thoughts*** is one of the most difficult things in life. It can, however, be done if one practices hard and regularly. (Happiness Is Divine: p.9)

A great number of people go on believing constantly that their failure in life is the result of some kind of failing on the part of someone else. Often one also goes on expressing ill-will and ***resentment*** towards others without their involvement in any kind of malicious act against his/her. Even if one has failed on account of one's own mistakes or inadequacy, one may start believing that the failure was caused because of others. One of my well-known persons who worked hard throughout his life and tried to provide as much as he could to all his children. But one of his sons usually failed in classes when he was a student in high school. For his failures, he often accused the father for not providing this or that. The father would often converse with me and sometimes relate the story of his children as he confided in me. Listening to his story I came to conclude that the only lasting answer to such ***resentment*** is 'forgiveness' and properly understanding the accusing person.

However, sometimes it takes a lot of time to forgive others as we don't really try to understand why the other has been acting so indifferently. Besides, the act of forgiveness also involves forgetting one's own wounds. It needs a lot of courage and kindness to forget one's own injuries. It also needs time to do so. As most people don't have it, so they are not able to do so. Consequently, ***resentment*** persists in our lives. If we really want gratification, peace and happiness in our lives, we must ***practice patience*** and ***forgiveness***. It is the only answer to cast away one's resentment in life.

The feeling of ***guilt*** is a strong mental-shackle that goes on keeping us constantly disturbed. Anyone who harbours the guilt feeling, can never get peace until he/she removes the cause that created such a feeling. If you try to repress the guilt feeling, it may fade away for sometime. However, it would stay there to torture the person who possesses it. A continued guilt feeling can work like a deadly poison and go on disturbing the person for long.

In this context, I recall some instances where people contained guilt feelings for years even though those persons tried hard to compensate it by doing some good work for others. One of my close friends from Sri Lanka, working with me in Nigeria in a University, accidently killed a ten years old local girl while he was driving his car. The girl came on the road all of a sudden and met the accident. Although, my friend paid quite a handsome money to the girls' parents in compensation, he could not forget that he killed a girl. During my long stay in that town in Africa, I met him many times, but each time he expressed his remorse and guilt feelings towards that happening. Although, he had paid a lot of money to the family of the dead girl, and often went to see her parents to console them, he still contained the guilt feelings.

Yes, it is difficult to forget the guilt feelings, but there is a way to extinguish such feelings. It is resolve not to repeat it even though if something is done inadvertently. One must resolve to make amends if possible and seek forgiveness of the person against whom the wrong has been done. Then forgetting it is the only way to let that painful feeling go for ever. If some of these things are done, the wound, lurking in one's mind, may get healed gradually and the ***guilt*** feeling may completely wash away.

Worry is the most common hang up with the people and a thin stream of fear constantly going on trickling in people's minds. In fact, it is 'fear' that usually cause worry in our minds. Jiddu Krishnamurti, the great philosopher from India, analyses the cause of worry quite lucidly. He reflects that it is the mind that creates fear and on that account worry ultimately erupts in our minds. Krishnaurti reckons that thinking involves words. One cannot in fact think without words, without symbols and images. Most of time these sorts of images are caused because of our prejudices, because of our previous knowledge and anxieties of mind. When these anxieties are projected upon the fact, fear comes out of that. When fear is projected, it causes worry which in turn go on hurting someone even without any intentions. Thus, several consequences of worry could be seen.

Just for example, when someone's parents are worrying for their son's coming back home late from a theatre or from any recreation place, they go on worrying for him. Different kinds of thoughts invade their minds. They may think least their son should meet any accident on the road while driving his motor cycle or bike or he developed some other kind of problem which has made him reach home late. Until he reaches home, they are tortured by worry. During this period of worry ridden mind, if someone asks them anything, they are likely to speak very curtly, which may cause troubles for them later on. Thus, worry is such a hang-up for a man, that it always causes problems.

Jiddu Krishnamurti holds that mind can be free from fear only when it is capable of looking at the fact without translating it and without giving it a name or label. It is very difficult as the feelings, reactions and anxieties possessed by someone, are instantly identified by the mind and given a word. Is it possible not to identify such a feeling and look at that feeling without naming it? Perhaps, it is difficult and it is because of that, that people usually indulge in hurting others without much cause.

I better try to explain it with a certain example. Suppose, a family has only one child. The parents usually go on worrying for him/her all the time. The mother and the father go on worrying for him in different ways. One may worry for his health and the other for his conduct. Later on, when he is grown up and starts going to school, they both may worry about his studies. Thus, worry is a big factor that always causes problems for anyone who cradles it.

Worry and fear often go hand in hand. Where there is any kind of worry, there is fear as well. Is it possible to identify a feeling such as fear of ghost or someone will certainly inflict losses to us etc.? Krishnamurti holds that fearing for something without naming it, usually creates problems. The moment you give a name to that, you call 'fear', you strengthen it. But the moment 'you can look at that feeling without terming it, you will see that it withers away.' So, if one wants to be free from fear, it is imperative that one understands the whole process of terming, of naming the images and projecting symbols. One can be free from fear when one has self-knowledge. That is the beginning of real knowledge and true happiness as well. The basic truth about worry is that most fears about it are unfounded. Several people go on worrying about their health, about their children and about so many things, but quite often nothing happens. Vast majorities of feared tragedies probably never take place.

Besides, if you go on worrying about them, nothing you can do to prevent them by just worrying about them. On the contrary, worrying constantly would lead a person to absent-mindedness and ill-temper, which gives birth to so many maladies and other problems like accidents, conflicts and consequently lack of peace and happiness. To remove fear from one's mind, one should try to understand how much damage it can do to a person who goes on worrying for no solid reason for worrying. A senior doctor, named Charles Mayo reflects that, "Worry affects the circulation system, the heart, the glands and the whole nervous system. I have never known a man who died from overwork, but many who died from doubt."

However, there is some ***remedy to remove worry from your mind***. The easy way is just to divert oneself from it deliberately. Better go to play a game, go for a long walk along with your friend, see a movie, visit a loving friend, watch some interesting programme on television or do something like gardening. All such activities are far better than sitting at a place and brooding over unfounded things which are just creations of mind and keep you worried and dismayed. By changing one's setting, one can gradually change one's doleful mood. Haply the greatest medication for every sort of worry is the belief in God that He exists, and cares for us. A belief that He is always ready to help us, can gradually make us strong. Such thoughts can surely help us to forget worry to a great extent. No one's life is totally free from problems. If we know it, we can surely try forgetting worrying unnecessarily.

Stopping worrying can help us in two ways. One, that we can gradually become free of unnecessary ailments and two, that we can easily avoid hurting others during such spells of worry as during such times we are likely to hurt someone who may be so close to us. So, let us try to dispel it from our minds, for it may surely create sever problems for us.

Jealousy is another great roadblock in our lives. Most people who suffer from jealousy are those who cultivate complexes in their minds. One who contains it, will go on keeping it and will never be able to live peacefully. And without peace, one cannot live happily. Most people have a habit of comparing themselves with those who lead a successful and flourishing lives. When one compares oneself with others it leads to justifying one's own inadequacies against the strong points of character in others. Consequently, it gives vent to jealousy. It is also quite true and unfortunate as well that people, who hail from a particular environment, are more used to compare themselves with others. As a result, they suffer more with complexes than those who belong to a wider environment and their thinking and living habits are quite different. We can easily explain it with some suitable examples.

While I was working in Africa around forty years back, I had a great opportunity to meet different sorts of people coming from different lands. There I found that people usually hailing from Asia region and especially those who had come there quite recently, would greatly suffer from complexes. They would go on comparing themselves with the others who had been there for a long time. Those who had been living for a pretty long time, possessed almost every kind of amenity. Many of them usually possessed expensive cars and lived in good houses allocated by the University or government counting their seniority and position in the University or college. Most new comers did not possess many of such things and they often started comparing themselves with the affluent. Consequently, complexes developed which resulted in jealousy against the people of their own country.

Hopefully, patience and courage to take challenges would have solved the problems of all those who would sit in the evening at some place and indulged in gossips, vomiting jealousy against their own countrymen. However, those who were thoughtful could overcome their feelings of jealousy and worked hard to attain good positions. But those who were simply braggers, continued with their complexes and as a result landed themselves many a times into varied kinds of problems.

Most persons who suffer from jealousy have their own reasons to support it. A good job with good monthly income, a good and cozy house, an attractive physique, a comely countenance and academic excellence possessed by others easily become the cause of jealousy for those who don't possess all that. The only good way to avoid jealousy against others is to avoid such feelings by having patience. We have already reflected on the importance of practicing patience in some earlier chapter. If one possesses patience, one may not indulge in comparison and consequently stay free from jealousy.

Jiddu Krishnamurti also reflected that '***comparison, condemnation*** and ***identification***' are the sources of creating disturbance to any human mind. When our minds are distracted due to constant comparison and condemnation, jealousy stays with us for a long time. How can one live peacefully when the mind possesses disturbing thoughts that are full of jealousy? It is therefore, necessary to cast away the ideas that lead our minds to cultivate jealousy or complexes. It does not matter much if someone possesses more wealth than what I have. It does not make any difference if someone is having an expensive car than I possess. It does also not make any difference if someone has a more beautiful wife comparatively. A cool look at the things that disturb our minds, would help us to a great extent to live peacefully and happily.

The *Bhagwat Gita* contains something for us that may satisfy us in different ways and help us keep cool when such nasty thoughts invade our minds. It says:

Thy right is to work only; but never to the fruits thereof.
Be thou not the producer of (thy) actions;

neither let thy attachment be towards inaction.
—Gita Chapter II Verse 47.

If we understand the above verse clearly, we don't need to involve in thinking about others or about their wealth and thus stay away from cultivating ill-thoughts in our minds. Our duty is to act and not to think about the fruits of that act. If we can cultivate such a dispassionate attitude in life, it would be easy for us to forget jealousy or to contain any nasty thoughts.

Nobody's life is free from problems. The world has been going on like that and will go on further also. Why should then we complain about things which we don't have and others possess them? In fact, life is full of challenges. That is what it is. The greatest challenge of life lies in detachment with things. If we don't possess that, we go on indulging in worry, anxiety or such ill-thoughts. That constantly go on distracting us from the right path. Therefore, let us dispel our doubts, resentments and guilt feelings that push us to the realm of worry and jealousy. Let us then try hard to replace all such mental barriers with strength and endless joy. Those who live with doubt and confusion, are bound to suffer from short-sightedness. Those who are religious fanatics, they also suffer on account of such a mental makeup. Religious fanaticism or any other kind of extremism, excludes one from having a clear vision of the world. If an individual's vision is blurred, his/her mind is transported away from the freedom as his/her thinking is conditioned. Such an individual is likely to suffer from emotional problems.

However, if one extends love to all, it leads to end the narrowness of heart. Consequently, his/her vision is widened, heart becomes compassionate and leads the person to cultivate forgiveness and providing right understanding. Only that kind of love can bestow true happiness, which is devoid of any kind of conditioning, whether religious, cultural or linguistic. But if one possesses any sort of mental barriers, he/she will surely dwell in confusion and turmoil. Can a man seek any true happiness when he/she is surrounded by mental barriers? Mind should always be kept free from any sort of barriers so that it could see clearly. In fact, freedom of mind and happiness go together. But if it is conditioned by any road blocks, it can neither enjoy the present, nor future and always dwells in confusion.

When we talk of religious fanaticism, we don't mean Christ, Swami Yogananda, Sri Ram Krishna, St. Joan or Swami Vivekananda. They possessed illimitable love for Him and their belief in God was endless. They had no any doubts in that respect. At the same time, they also loved mankind deeply and ardently. Their examples are not parallel to any human beings in the world. St. Joan's love for God is a unique story of a human being. She displayed great attachment toward Him that it is difficult to imagine. Meera's love for Krishna is equally great. In fact, we cannot compare any of these God loving people as far as their love for God is concerned. Their examples are really supreme. They also did not possess any kind of resentment, jealousy or ill-feelings for humans. On the contrary, they always displayed great love, care and respect for each and every one. It made them enormously great and happy as well.

Before closing this chapter that we had started with the issue, 'if you hurt someone, it is likely that he/she would also react against it', we would like to discuss about ***ego*** or ***complexes*** a little bit more at this juncture though we have discussed it earlier too. To me, the term ***ego*** looks quite related to the issue 'hurting others and not expecting them to hurt you back.'

In the chain of discussing barriers to human mind, inspiring to react and hurt people, the role of ***ego*** is great. It usually keeps human beings far away from their true happiness and takes them to the realm of jealousy, frustration and disappointment, indulging them with enmity against others and even with their own kith and kin. At this point, we would like to examine it from slightly a different angle.

Ego is not only a kind of ill-feeling possessed by human beings, it is also a driving force for them to make them move ahead. Yes, people are loaded with proud feelings about something they possess relatively more and better than others—something like, that they work harder and try to go forward than others in the race of gaining wealth or material things and things of amenities. It also works quite differently especially when certain people working as seniors at some place. They usually reckon that whatever they do, think or decide, is always right. There is a very popular saying in this respect. Lots of people wont to say it inadvertently when comparing someone's conduct with a particular person. They say, "The boss is always right and when he is wrong, he is right too."

Quite often ego works against others and helps creating enemies. If someone is comparatively more handsome, or somebody's sons or daughters are in a high position in a private sector or in a government department, or if one has a good status in a private company or in a government department, one may display ego in several ways. Once I came across someone special at a particular time of my age. He was working in a very senior position in some important security department of the government. I met that person when he must have been around 35 to 40 years old.

Once we four-five friends were sitting in a coffee-house just after our office time and were trying to indulge inadvertently in gossips and also to learn more about some important news of the day we considered significant. As we were discussing something relating the security of the county at that time, the friend whom I had met not very far away as far as months had gone by, just got up from his seat and started thumping his chest wildly with his right hand, talking loudly and opposing one of the persons sitting in the group. The discussion was going about, "How the government maintains the security of the country against spying by the other countries, especially by the neighbouring ones". The proud officer who stood up from his seat all of a sudden, said to the person who was unfolding his knowledge about the way security was maintained in the country, "You know nothing about it. Ask me I will tell you how it is done as I am a senior officer in the Government security department."

As soon as he said so loudly and thumping his chest forcefully, the other fellow told him politely, "Please sit down. Don't be so excited. You don't need to tell us how the security is maintained. We also know about it quite extensively." Listening to that, the proud officer lost his temper and started shouting loudly, "You know nothing about the security. Don't talk rubbish." All that was enough to indulge in a fight which was averted with great persuasion and difficulty. They calmed down after a lot of persuasion. Therefore, ***ego*** may also lead hurting others and creating great problems for people who cradle it.

Being proud of oneself about something you possess in abundance is good, but to exhibit that quality in public as a show and to indicate your superiority over others, is a sign of possessing false dignity. 'Who cares for your richness or your beautiful countenance or possessing a Mercedes car?' They belong to you and not to me so I am also not disturbed by your possessing all that. I care for you only if you are kind, caring and loving to others. I do care for you if you are helpful to others in their dire needs. I care for you and love you if you are a man of words and always keep your promises. I do care for you when you stand for people when they are in dire need on account of certain natural calamities or any other reason. Such people, who take care of others without any returns, are honoured and loved by all without restraint and without fail. They are the real jewels of the society as they know what kind of help is needed by the people and what is best for them at particular occasions.

The four mental hang-ups, ***self-doubt, resentment, guilt*** and ***worry*** indicated by Dr. Peale and two more, ***jealousy*** and ***ego*** that I added, are certainly great disturbing factors to any human being if any of them is cradled in the mind. Being nasty and disturbing, they easily transports a human being to the land of great turmoil, bringing him/her various sorts of problems, constant disturbance and consequently making him/her totally unhappy and dismayed. Then how to be free from them so that during the spells of anyone of them, your mind stays cool and undisturbed and doesn't hurt others leading to get several problems.

Perhaps the ways suggested during our discussions, if followed whole heartedly, would be quite helpful to keep you within your control and help you avoid hurting others even if you are hurt, insulted or disturbed by others. Let us try some of them when we get disturbed on account of worry or guilt or by possessing self-doubts. I strongly hold that Jiddu Krishnamurti has suggested a wonderful way to keep us calm and controlled by removing all thoughts from our minds and stay at peace. Though it may look difficult to do so in the beginning at times, but if we go on trying, gradually we may make our mind free from any thoughts and attain peace. We can also cultivate such a habit by regular practice and ensure our happiness. Where peace resides, happiness also lives.

Jiddu Krishnamurti also reflected that ***comparison, condemnation and identification*** are the great sources of bring disturbance to us. When our minds are distracted due to comparison and condemnation, it is quite natural that jealousy may spring up in our minds and hearts, making us restless and extremely disturbed. That becomes the source of great disturbance and make us react or hurt others without any reason. Consequently, we too react to that hurt as it is quite natural to react against a hurt or insulted by someone. How can one live peacefully when the mind possesses disturbing thoughts on account of jealousy? How can we stop hurting others as we possess complexes and are badly affected by our resentment and anxiety created by somebody's bad conduct or uneven behaviour?

At such occasions it is necessary to cast away the ideas that lead our minds to cultivate jealousy or any kind of complexes. It does not matter much if someone possesses more wealth than what we have. It also does not make any difference to you if someone possess an expensive car than what you have. How does it make any difference to me if someone is more handsome or is better looking than what I am? The only way to stay calm relating all such things, is to look at these things with a cool mind and stay undisturbed. That would help us to a great extent live peacefully and happily. So, avoid living with mental confusion as that leads the mind to react against others, which is detrimental to our own happiness.

When Gandhi Ji was thrown out of the first class compartment from the train while travelling in South Africa as he was an Indian, instead of hurting anyone orally or attempting to inflict any pain to those who threw him down the train, he pledged to work in his own country to get freedom from the British who had thrown him out of the train compartment. The British were also ruling in India for several years at that time. It was such a moral and spiritual abiding pledge, with a strong determination that he worked very hard to get his own country free from the British rule. It was also a kind of reply to what the British did to him in South Africa. Though Gandhi did not seem to take his hurt personal, he too could not forget it and replied against the British in a different but it was much tougher and harder reply to them for what they did to him years back. So, most people don't forget their hurt feelings but use different ways to hurt back at times. It is true to a large extent, that a person who is hurt, cannot digest it easily. However, their paths to inflict pain and hurting back may be different. But should a person always need to hurt back? It is the main question at this juncture. I believe there are surely different ways to react against somebody's hurting you. Perhaps, that way could be quite different but sure it could be more comforting and consoling.

If we look at the lives of Socrates, Buddha and Christ dispassionately, we find that they have so many things in common. They all fought to stay on the right path, fully implicit with spirituality, sincerity and benevolence. All the three when came to end of their lives, they tried to forgive those who actually hurt them.

Socrates sincere efforts brought his countrymen spiritual and mental benefits as he taught them what was right and how to reach that with a reflective and logical mind.

The Buddha and Christ have their own tales which strongly tell us how we could perpetually follow the right path and attain spirituality to gain endless happiness. If one goes on trying hard, one may finally choose forgiveness against hurt and may never attempt to inflict any pain to others even if one is hurt, insulted or assaulted. Yes, we all cannot lead life like Mahatma Gandhi, Christ or Buddha, but we can certainly try to avert an odd situation by our appropriate attitude and proper way of thinking which are so important to teach us how to deflect the pain and avoid hurting others back when they hurt us.

But, it is also true that until we forgive, we stay locked in our pain: Without forgiving we remain tethered to the feeling or the person.

6

When We Forgive, We Take Back Control of Our Own Fate Forgiveness is the Best Form of Self-interest

The idea of forgiveness is great but it is very difficult to cultivate it. Anger is such an element of human nature that it resides quite close to a person most of the time. As soon as one has a chance to vent it, one vomits it without giving it a second thought. For quite a number of people it is very convenient to hurt others for their own fancy, stupidity or whatever reason may be. So, many people, at times, are wont to hurt others even for their own enjoyment or pleasure. The idea of forgiveness is far away from such people, though it could be the best form of self-interest. There are several reasons that don't allow a person to forgive.

It has been observed that many people go on keeping ill-will against others for they think they have been offended by them many a times. They keep ill-will against people as they don't like them on account of their own prejudices and complexes. This sort of process goes on and on for quite a long time without thinking or trying to forget it. As a result our lives are usually filled in with hatred and dislike but we never think about forgiving people who have done something wrong inadvertently or on account of any serious reason. That never makes us happy.

Customarily it is quite difficult to perceive the idea of forgiveness. Most people don't think about it closely. Some also think that forgiving others may mean some kind of weakness on the part of the forgiving person. Therefore, the thought of forgiving is pushed aside. Forgiving is also truly very difficult as it needs a lot of courage and sane thinking. If someone has learnt how to forgive others for their mistakes or faults, he/she will always reckon it very important and try continuing it as it definitely provides peace, harmony as well as colossal happiness. But it does not happen commonly.

It is so unfortunate that when any difficult situation of a strange nature comes to our lives where we need to forgive others, we normally don't think about forgiving. It is a basic truth that when we are surrounded with difficulties, we don't like to recollect our strength as we usually feel fatigued and our strength seem to be worsening. We feel that we ae lacking something, we are lost—completely lost amid commotion. Under such circumstances, we usually lose temper, accusing others and start hating others for none of their faults. That gives us the idea of taking revenge. That is the time when the thought of retaliation creeps into our minds making us restless and inspiring us to act the way which would give us satisfaction by hurting others. It is, in fact, that moment of our life when we are completely far away from right kind of thinking—devoid of hope and light but full of anguish and desirous to take revenge, unable to do what is right.

The *Bhagwat Gita* unfolds such a situation very aptly when Arjuna refuses to fight as he gets confused and frustrated by looking at his own kinsmen all round him in the battle against whom he has to fight. He gets totally muddled and refuses to fight as he is filled with remorse and is distressed. He is not able to decide whether to fight or not. At that occasion, Sri Krishna advises him consolingly, that he needs to cast away his delusion, needs to think with reason and be ready to fight, for delusion always leads to confusion. But Arjuna is not ready to fight as his heart is totally filled with remorse. It is the moment when Sri Krishna enlightens him with some very inspiring words encouraging him to fight as it is his duty to start fighting at that moment.

Sri Krishna unfolds him:

"From anger proceeds delusion; "from delusion confused Memory; from confused memory the destruction of Reason; from destruction of Reason he perishes."

Listening to these words, Arjuna starts to think carefully as he feels inspired and becomes ready to fight against his own kinsmen as they are unjust and devoid of good. Under most circumstances, we try to run away from taking right decision like Arjuna, and refuse to act the way we need to act. Thus, forgiving is equally difficult when we are hurt. We simple think of hurting and destroying others in some way if they have done something wrong towards us.

The Weak Moments

We all have weak moments at several times in life and consequently get confused and doleful. Even saints and holy people have experienced such moments in their lives and as a result get agitated and frustrated. Jesus Christ too had such moments in his life when he was being badly whipped by the Roman soldiers and conducted to the Cross but he kept calm and thus controlled his frustration. Meera had to implore Sri Krishna several times when she was in great distress on account of others' atrocities. Sri Rama Krishna, during his distressed moments in life, went on imploring the Goddess Kali for several days, insisting upon Her to feed him or he would not eat. But in spite of the thwarting circumstances and hard circumstances, these holy people somehow tried hard to transcend themselves and mounted a stage where they got peace and happiness. Therefore, though we all get week moments in life, but only those who can think adequately and rightly, keep patience and courage, can transcend to such situations and attain the stage which is full of tranquility. Those who cannot keep patience and courage, can never do so as their thinking is blocked either by revengeful feelings or distrust.

If we try to turn the pages from history, we can get several examples of the nature when religious and wise men and women suffered on account of others' mistakes, meanness and revengeful demeanour. In spite of that these kind and good people never reacted against anyone who inflicted pain or injury to them. Buddha simply forgave Kunda when he came to know that he was offered poisonous food by him. He could think properly and therefore, did not react against his killer as he had discovered that Kunda gave him that food inadvertently. Is it not really difficult to forgive one's own killer? Both the Buddha and Christ did forgive the people who gave them death. Who would do so when he/she is at the gates of death? I reckon, only those people can think of forgiveness, who can control their anger and reflect sanely. They can reach the right judgment.

There are many more examples besides the above when people had hard times but they did not react to take revenge against their tormentors or against the people who inflicted pain to them by their cruelties. They understood it clearly that falling into revengeful acts would simply mean stooping down to a low level of thinking which would lead them to demean their souls and take them to the peace-less stage of mind. Thus, in spite of great danger to life, good people generally don't react adversely but keep patience and courage and try to reach the right state of thinking. That helps them to concluding, what is most appropriate for them. They usually stay calm and try to be contended, keep courage, thinking let it happen what should happen. Let me support this with some appropriate examples.

When Vivekananda came to America to take part in the Religious Conference to be held in Chicago, his belongings were lost there.

He had nothing left for him, not even his clothes that he had brought from India. Nether he had a place to stay nor any money to spend on anything. Once, while he was sleeping in an empty goods train compartment, he was roughly treated by the police considering him a vagabond and forced him to get out of the compartment. He did not lose courage or faith at that occasion and went on contemplating to find other better ways so that he could participate in the conference.

Meera's story also unfolds something of that nature. When she was harassed and tortured by the Rana, her own near relative, she did not react to that but went on imploring Sri Krishna for help. Instead of getting scared or agitated, she kept herself drowned in Krishna's love and devotion so that she could forget all the ills done against her, but never reacted against her tormentors. (Unparalleled Love, pp-45-49) Only those who are really good, dutiful and responsible and have full faith in God, can always try stay calm. They usually don't get panicky and never react against anything circumstance or person. Since they think in a different direction and are strong within, they stay cool and act with courage.

What about the military or police personnel. Every time when there is trouble at the boarder or whenever any infiltrator sneaks through the boarders into the country, or riots break in a city or town, they always stand against all such activities and fight against the people who create problems without caring for their own lives. All such exercises are selfless and to discharge one's duty honestly as well sincerely. The military personal who always stand guarding the boarders of the country, never tell their seniors or anyone else, even their own nearest relatives that they are being used by the seniors or the government and their lives are always at stake. They go on fighting the odd circumstances dutifully and honestly at the cost of their own life.

Though *week moments* come to everyone in life, but those who are really strong and can think appropriately implicit with reason, always stand right. Only such people don't fear any grim or uneven circumstances and withstand all the atrocities without fearing or reacting against anything or anyone, facing problems fearlessly.

Picking Out the Right Path

Perhaps, it is a God's gift to humans and all living beings that whenever there are odd circumstances, except some, most people usually like to fight against them and try avert such odd situations to keep themselves safe and hearty. A very simple example would support the above view. Once around twenty years back when I was travelling to a certain place by my own car in my own State in India, all of a sudden I realised that something was wrong with the car. When I stopped the car, I found that one of its tires was flat. Unfortunately, I did not have all the necessary tools to replace the tire. So I could only stand there on the roadside waiting for someone to help me. Since it was quite a frequently used road by people, there was fairly good traffic on the road. I therefore, stood there waiting for God-sent assistance or a person who would help me. My lady (my wife) was rather a bit restless at my standing and waiting there. She asked me several times to do something rather than just stand and wait there fruitlessly. In between she also went on commenting, "How long would you stand here to wait for help?" I had only one answer for that, "Let us wait for sometime more." Then after keeping quiet for sometime, she would repeat the same question, how long would we go on waiting there.

I had nothing else but to wait there until I get some help. In the meantime I was also planning for several alternatives of help, like getting some help to tow the car to a safe place or to a mechanic. I also started thinking about some others ways to get the tire changed. However, I did not lose courage and at the same time and also continued planning for alternatives to continue my journey. If I had lost hope and drowned in despair, I would have been broken down at that small problem. It was quite surprising that after half an hour a vehicle passed by us. The driver seemed to be a compassionate person. He stopped his vehicle and asked me, "Any problem?" I said, "Yes, my tire is flat and I have not all the tools to replace it." Listening to me, he got down from his vehicle and helped me change the tire as he possessed all the needed tools and instruments.

Thus, when we get difficult circumstances in life many a time, we just don't stand or wait at a place for long, weeping and wondering what to do then. Instead, we like to fight against that situation without blaming others for the odd circumstances that have befallen on us all of a sudden. If one starts accusing others for his/her odd situations, it would be like hurting others for no reason whenever we are in difficulty due to any reasons. Many people always go on accusing others only for their own shortcomings. I have provided several examples of that nature to the readers for their kind reference a little earlier in some earlier chapters in the book.

Arrogance Powered by Ego

Some people are aggressively arrogant and go on hurting others with their bigheaded attitude, inflicting pain and disrespect to others by their haughty demeanour. I provided one suitable example of that nature when I discussed about the behaviour of a friend, who while sitting with a group of friends, commented quite arrogantly against one of the friends that "Not you but only I know about how security services function." He also commented that what he (the other friend) had been talking about the security for a long time, was not correct. Such reflections simply display someone's arrogance and ego which always bring remorse later on and repay the person adversely. We may quote a few great examples of that nature from the legends and history that tell us how the arrogant persons finally fell and were punished by the people or God for their bad conduct and arrogant behaviour against others.

There is no better example of that kind than the legendry Ravana in the holy book, *Ramayana*. It was Ravana's arrogance implicit with ego that he waged war against Sri Ram after taking away his wife Sita forcefully from the *Ashoka Vatika* where she was living with Sri Rama at that time. Sri Rama had opted to go to forest for fourteen years to fulfill his father's promise given to one of his mothers. Those who have read *Ramayana,* know the story well, can easily understand all what resulted on account of Ravana's conduct which was terribly unworthy of a good king. Even when Ravana's father and mother tried to explain to him that he was totally wrong and unjust, he refused to follow their advice and went on behaving in an arrogant manner, which simply resulted in the destruction of his entire demon clan, his children and family.

Similar kind of happenings can be revealed by history in which arrogant rulers without caring for helping mankind, went on ruining hundreds of lives by their atrocities. Hitler and Napoleon are the best examples of that nature. They both did not care for others but to obtain satisfaction of their own egos and went on killing hundreds and thousands of people in the war they waged against the innocent people. Arrogance powered with ego is a double sin in the sense that it only leads people to march on the wrong path which ultimately brings their destruction and demise. Yes, people react when they suffer or are attacked by calamities. We all fail at times and are unable to do what is needed but someone affected with that kind of situation must think twice to do wrong to the persons as at times things happen without their desire or any intentions. The best way at such occasions would be to stay hopeful and think in the right direction as well as obtain right means to fulfill the requirements.

Staying Hopeful

At this juncture I am reminded of a strange situation that befell in Buddha's life immediately after he attained Enlightenment. The whole night, just before reaching the stage of Enlightenment, he went on viewing the scenes from his past lives. When the two-third of that night had passed, he had a vison of light which was to have reached the state of Enlightenment. He started enjoying it until dawn and adored it fully, completely drowned in it. As soon as he ended enjoying that stage, Mara (God of Death) suddenly appeared before him and asked him a very strange and difficult question. Mara said, "Yes, you are now enlightened but what is its advantage to you? Listening to Mara, Buddha did not get disturbed, neither he threshed him, saying, 'Ok, I got it, I am happy with that. What have to do with my Enlightenment Mara? You just get away.' Instead he went to meditate for a few minutes to find its answer. After a few minutes when he opened his eyes, he told Mara, "If even five people are benefitted by my teachings and get enlightened, my purpose of attaining Enlightenment is fulfilled." Listening to that, Mara instantly disappeared from his presence.

So, sane and disciplined persons keep patience and always control their anger. Neither, they exert their ill-will before others, nor hurt anyone. If one is disciplined and can control one's temper, one would never display any bad temper or show anger to anyone, as he/she knows to follow the right path. Such people always try to stay hopeful and never like to indulge in violence or hurt others for any reason even if they are hurt by others. In that respect we have unparalleled example of Mahatma Gandhi, who when assaulted by the British and was thrown out of the first class compartment of the train in South Africa as he was an Indian, he never shouted or hurled any bad words to those who had disrespected him. Yes, if he reacted, he chose a right path which was absolutely appropriate in two ways—one that he did not resort to any violence even later on, and that his path helped his countrymen to get freedom from the British rule. How did he reach that decision when normally most people are unable to think properly in such an agitated situation? Haply he was endowed with a kind of temperament that led him to find a better solution for his indignation. And there could not be a better resolution than what he took at that occasion.

Could we all try to reach the stage of better thinking when surrounded by ill-thoughts and keep patience to follow only the right path? If we can, we all will be able to avert a number of problems that encounter us after we react to them. In order to reach the dominion implicit with love and compassion we would always need to choose a particular way of life. Sri Rama, Krishna chose the way which was full of faith in God. When Meera chose to reach Sri Krishna as her life's goal, she went on following it in spite of the atrocities her own in-laws regularly inflicted on her. Sri Rama always believed in social values and practiced them in His whole life in spite of great difficulties He encountered throughout life. Guru Nanak Dev Ji equally suffered many a time during the course of his life, but he never deviated from the right path.

The truth is that life become a companion of one's thoughts. Most people keep in drowning in them most of the time and become like their thoughts. If good thoughts are cultivated, it results in leading a good and straight life, but if one usually stays in the company of bad thoughts, one is likely to resort to bad acts and consequently suffer accordingly. When people commit suicide, they are not able to rise above their failures and disappointments. But I have also seen people, who have risen above their odd circumstances and mounted to a great height in life. Thus, the way of life one contemplates to lead, becomes one's way to live.

If one has the habit of reading good literature and good books that are good to provide inspiration, it is quite likely that one may choose better ways to live. When we read profusely, we find many good examples of people who never lost courage or gave up when surrounded by difficult circumstances. Sir Winston Churchill is one of the good examples in that respect. Swami Vivekananda, Paramahansa Yogananda, Mahatma Gandhi, Atal Bihari Bajpai, Shyama Prasad Mukerje and Dr. Abdul Kalam are some of the best examples in that respect. We have already reflected in this respect on the lives of Socrates and Christ. All these people always fought their odd circumstances and reached a great height in their lives. It is therefore very imperative to believe in good things and lead only the best way in one's life.

Controlling Mind

At times it is really difficult to penchant criticism that relates the self. When one is exposed to self-criticism, one tries to be defensive and usually discovers ways to justify the actions one has followed. Most people go on arguing and providing defensive reasons to justify the ways followed by them. The best way at such occasions is to leave defensive attitude and accept plainly one's shortcomings. It will always be fruitful to keep one's own principles rather than unusually be defensive for our own faults. One of the best ways I reckon, is to stand for oneself and speak well and clearly for the self, both inwardly as well as confidently.

Acquiring Generosity

To acquire all such confidence one has to be generous for others in recognising their qualities and abilities. It is also imperative that one is generous for one's own self too. For if you go on talking or thinking of your own shortcomings, people may take you as a babbler having no knowledge of the self and the world. It would always be better to think what one possesses rather than what one does not have. At times, it is really difficult for some people to accept themselves as they are and they go on talking low about themselves. Such a way of thinking may shatter their self-confidence. It does not help anyone in anyway. Consequently, it conducts one to the region of so many mental or psychological problems and they go on assuming their lacking. That may easily take one to various sorts of failures as one's self-confidence has been shattered. But if one contemplates about one's qualities, though limited, it provides confidence. Everyone of us has plenty to give to others in so many ways provided we have confidence in our ownself.

It is a plain truth that we all are unsuccessful at different times in our lives and feel dejected and usually shrink back at such occasions. Often we talk about our ills, mistakes and wrong doings without thinking that the persons to whom we are relating our woeful story would judge us low or they may not be concerned at all to know all such details about our failures. That also does not help us in any way. Rather, we also start thinking that we are not worthy to do anything. At time a sincere friend may go on listening our woeful story and may sympathise with us too, but how long would he go on listening to all that rubbish that has no meaning to him or to you? We often do so to get others' sympathies so that our woeful state of mind could get redeemed. The truth it that nothing of that kind happens. The more we discuss about our shortcomings and failures, the more weak we feel inside and our self-confidence is gradually shattered. The only way to get rid of such a situation is not to invite such thoughts. It will be further good at such occasions to try forget such things and stop inviting the thoughts that go on renewing our pain.

Building Self-confidence

Let us always try thinking to acquire our lost self-esteem and confidence. Better forget all sorts of adversities and buy sometime for yourself. It is the basic truth that we all need sometime for us too, but many of us don't know it. "One of my good friends would always ask to leave her alone when she felt disgusted on account of a hard situation created by others." (**"Happiness is Divine"** p.62) It is always good to have a good friend to whom one can talk about one's problems. We all have good and bad times in life, but when we lose someone who was our most dear one, we feel wracked. It is the right moment to seek the company of the good friends so that we can share of our pain with them and comforted.

Heart-touching Prayers

For such occasions heart touching prayers are the best treatment. Soren Kierkegaard says, "The function of prayer is not to influence God, but rather to change the nature of the one who prays." Thus, by regular prayers one can go on changing one's distorted self, and gradually collect courage and become confident about own, self. It is one of the several ways to acquire self-confidence, courage and peace of mind.

When Roman soldiers were conducting Christ to the Cross and His hands and feet were nailed, He suffered tremendous pain during all that tormenting. But to get redeemed from that pain, He constantly prayed. Socrates suffered a lot when he drank hemlock. He too must have kept himself engaged in praying to redeem from his pain. All these God fearing people prayed hard to seek His blessings to get free from their pain. At this point I am reminded of a real life story of a lady who worked with me in a college around thirty-five years back when I headed that college in India after my return from Africa. She developed cancer just two years back (from 2016) in her abdomen. Her loving children immediately took care of her as her husband had died long back. She stayed on chemotherapy for quite a long time. It is quite a painful treatment and one's hair also falls down during that treatment. Her suffering was great but she withstood it for two years until she was fully recovered. Just imagine how those two years would have been passed by her in constant fear of death, pain and anguish. She told me all that when I got a chance to visit. She narrated that during her most painful moments, she would always resort to prayers and tried to forget herself. That gave her lot of self-confidence and relieved her from the terrible physical pain. Thus, prayers are surely one of the greatest sources to collect courage and regenerate self. Prayers enriched with forgiveness for our mistakes offered deliberately or inadvertently, can bring us tremendous comfort, joy and help us to come out from dismay and odd circumstances.

Keeping Nature's Company

However, there are ***other ways too besides the prayers*** to acquire confidence and recollect courage. For that one needs to look around oneself to seek happiness from nature. The beautiful world of nature is always there for us to give us incredible joy. A few days back I got a chance to go the Mt. Hood located around sixty-seventy miles away from Portland town in Oregon State in USA. One cannot imagine how nature can make one forget one's ailments and provide peace and comfort. The multicoloured flowers, the trickling brooks and regular flowing rivers by the side of the road deliver great message of tranquility and provide endless joy and happiness. It is the kind of ideal environment in nature that provides quietude which damps down the agitated moods and brings tranquility.

If we look at the nature's bounties, we find that at each step there are surprises for us. Nature gives us so many things each day without taking back anything from us. If nature can provide us plenty of things without any expectations, why we cannot forgive people without any strings. It is imperative to remember that forgiveness will certainly help us in forgetting our injuries by redeeming our shortsightedness and in return five us endless joy. (**Happiness is Divine** p.65) Nature always possess the right environment which may always lessen our mental pain whenever we suffer from it.

Rabindranath Tagore has rightly described an ideal environment usually created by a good setting. He writes:

"Where the mind is free:
Where the world has not broken up into fragments
by narrow domestic walls;
Where words come out from the depth of truth;
Where tireless striving stretches its arms towards perfection;
Where the clear stream of reason has not lost its way
into the dreary desert sand of dead habits;
Where the mind is led forward by Thee into ever
Widening thought and action;
Into the heaven of freedom...."
*(**Autobiography of a Yogi** p.308)*

Such a kind of environment was created by Rabindranath Tagore in a natural set up to run his *Visva-Bharti*, which has now grown to an international university. So, it is a primary need to change one's environment to keep one's mind cool and unaffected by emotional or any other sort of mental problem created when hurt on account of something and not able to forgive and forget.

Practicing Meditation

Considering the primary idea to forgive when hurt, besides prayers and changing environment by going into the lap of the nature, one may also cultivate a regular habit to meditate though for a few minutes, and try diverting one's attention from the odd situation, indulging in forgetting and forgiving. It also helps us to a great extent to calm down from our agitated state of mind and give us a glimpse to look on the other side of the things. Thus, making us divert our attention from the hurt or ill-treatment by someone leding us to resort to involve in some kind of aggression.

Meditation is not necessarily involving in prayers. At the same time, when one is involved in praying, he/she is also cultivating a habit of meditation. Both of these aspects of human endeavour are quite different, though many of us may hold that when one prays, one also involves in meditation. Therefore, if you involve in praying, don't deem yourself involved in meditation too. But the truth is that both the aspects are quite apart from each other.

Jiddu Krishnamurti does not at all talk about praying but of keeping one's mind free from incoming thoughts to attain peace and tranquility. He calls it a **thoughtlessness state of mind** in which it is devoid of any thoughts by gradually pulling them out from the mind. He also suggests that one does not need any training to keep the mind free from thoughts. One has to go on removing the incoming thoughts from one's mind so as to keep it completely free from thoughts. He considers only that state as the most meditative state of mind. Krishnamurti starts first anti-clockwise to begin with meditation. He unfolds:

> *Meditation is not following any system; it is not constant repetition and imitation. Meditation is not concentration. It is one of the favourite gambits of teachers of meditation to insist on their pupils learning concentration—that is fixing the mind on one thought and driving out all other thoughts. (**Happiness is Divine** p.67)*

Only when that stage of mind is reached, it is easy to make the mind free from every kind of thoughts. It is the stage which he calls **a thoughtless state of mind**.

The truth is that during meditation one becomes quite close to oneself. It is a way of recollecting the self in one whole from its scattered state which the person has reached due to numerous desires and attachments. A disturbed state of mind is such a state that leads one to create problems for the self as well for others. Therefore, meditation is a great help to anyone who cares for it practices it regularly even for a few minutes. We have also discussed about it to some extent in some previous chapter of the book.

Usually, meditation has been used by most people as a process to concentrate on things and issues requiring their immediate attention. Some people reckon that while they keep praying, they are meditating as well. Some dictionaries unfold it as 'sustained reflection' and also as 'the continuous application of mind to the completion of some religious truth, mystery or object of reverence.' The term meditation is applied to unfold different states of contemplation from which new notions may come up. (**Happiness is Divine** p. 66) During meditation one feels close to oneself and it is a most lucid procedure of recollecting the self in one whole from one' scattered state of mind. Thus, meditation is highly pragmatic and beneficial as well.

Quiet recently all over the world meditation is being used to reduce tension among humans as well as controlling high blood pressure which the doctors term as hypertension. So, many people who regularly involves with performing meditation have reported that it has benefitted them tremendously. Not only meditation helps changing the patterns of life to a great extent, it also assists in solving severe problems of life and reduce mental tension, which is caused at the time of loss of some very close relative on account of death or any other kind of misfortune.

Meditation implies watchfulness of the subjective as well as the objective worlds. It means seeing, watching and listening as well as being without any words. It is such a process in which mind is continually emptying itself of all sorts of thoughts and past experiences. Only then the self-consciousness flows freely, giving the individual immense pleasure, freedom and bliss. It is the most appropriate stage of mind when it can think of forgiving others for their misdeeds and insults done against you. Unless that stage of freedom of mind is attained by some of the aforesaid ways, that include meditation and prayers, one cannot think of forgiving anyone.

Meditative Process

There are several ways suggested to perform meditation but breathing is the only system in our body that is worth involuntary as well as voluntary and is often suggested by saints and those who recommend it as one of the best forms of meditation. Therefore, focusing on breath for our progressive well-being and good heatlth is an important aspect of meditation. In meditation, focusing on breathing can help us treat not simply the symptons, but also the causes of our suffering. In some forms of Buddhism focusing on breath is to clean out all the other stuff in the mind. Full belly breathing is recommended to reach the spot below the naval is considered to be the great source of energy. In the ***Heart of the Buddha's Teaching,*** Chinese Thich Nhat Hanh calls conscious breathing a perfect joy. He reflects, "When I discovered the Discourse on the Full awareness of Breathing, I felt was the happiest person on the earth. He further refers that focusing on breath in meditation as a means to enlightenment. The actual process of meditation through breathing is briefly given here below. (***Buddha Meditations: Lisa TE Sonne***-pp3032)

1. Breathing on a long breath, I know I am breathing in a long breath. Breathing out a long breath, I know I am breathing out a long breath.

2. Breathing in a sort breath, I know I am breathing in a short breath. Breathing out a short breath, I know I am breathing out a short breath.
3. Breathing in, I am aware of my whole body. Breathing out, I am aware of my whole body.
4. Breathing in, I calm my whole body. Breathing out, I calm my whole body.
5. Breathing in, I feel joyful. Breathing out, I feel joyful.
6. Breathing in, I feel happy. Breathing out, I feel happy.
7. Breathing in, I am aware of my mental formations. Breathing out, I am aware of my mental formations.
8. Breating in, I calm my mental formations. Breathing out, I calm my mental formations.
9. Breathing in, I am aware of my mind. Breathing out, I am aware of my mind.
10. Breathing in, I make my mind happy. Breathing out, I make my mind happy.
11. Breathing in, I concentrate my mind. Breathing out, I concentrate my mind.
12. Breathing in, I liberate my mind. Breathing out, I liberate my mind.
13. Breathing out, I observe the impermanent nature of all *dharmas*. Breathing out, I observe the impermanent nature of all *dharmas*.
14. Breathing in, I observe the disappearance of desires. Breathing out, I observe the disappearance of desires.
15. Breathing in, I observe the no-birth, no-death nature of all phenomena. Breathing out, I observe the no-birth, no-death nature of all phenomena.

16. Breathing in, I observe letting go. Breathing out, I observe letting go. (***Buddha Meditations: Lisa TE Sonne,*** p. 33-34)

The Buddha reflected that if complete awareness is developed and practiced continuously according to the directions given here above, 'the person, observing and practicing meditation through breathing, would be rewarded and benefitted immensely.'

If one can observe some of the beneficial ideas contained in the chapter relating keeping one's mind cool and controlled, away from disturbing ideas, one can gradually control one's mind and avoid unneneccasry skirmishes. Then one can develop the practice of continued patience. But with all that one surely needs forgiving attitude and forget the hurts inflicted by others. If it can be done, one can certainly advance towards forgiveness as it is the only best form of self-interest when one can really feel free from every kind of captivity. Let us finally talk a little more on the aspect of forgiveness.

❑❑❑

7

The Only Way to Experience Healing and Peace is to Forgive

We have already discussed at length that we don't easily forgive people and go on keeping in our minds the hurt inflicted on us by others. As there seems to be no immediate benefit from forgiving the wrong doers, the idea of forgiveness stays far away from us. Some people also consider that if they forgive others, they may be considered weak and helpless. So, the thought to forgive never comes to one's mind.

On the contrary, the truth is that considering forgiving others requires a lot of courage and proper thinking. We never think of it just like we invoke God's forgiveness and kindness for our own faults. Perhaps, most people reckon that forgiving is simply God's domain and duty towards us and only He can forgive us for our mistakes, crimes and deliberate or in-deliberate sins committed against others. So, the idea of forgiveness usually doesn't track through our minds.

At this juncture I would like to recall back Desmond Tutu's words when he was severely hurt at times when his father would beat his (Tutu's) mother ruthlessly. For a long time he too could not forget what his father did to his mother. I repeat his own words:

"If I dwell in those memories, I can feel myself wanting to hurt my father back, in the same ways of which I was incapable as a small boy. I see my mother's face and I see this gentle human being whom I loved so much and who did nothing to deserve the pain inflicted upon her."

He continues: "When I recall this story, I realise how difficult the process of forgiving truly is. Intellectually, I know my father caused pain because he was in pain. Spiritually, I know my faith tells me my father deserves to be forgiven as God forgives us all. But it is sill difficult. Even years later they can cause us fresh pain each time we recall them."

Forgiving Leads to Forgetting

It is a basic fact that we don't easily forget the painful thoughts very easily. I do remember how I was hurt by my own professor's treatment in the class. Though years later, when I went to see her to express my thanks to her for helping me in certain other matter at a different occasion, I did not seek her forgiveness for my own mistake made earlier when I came out of her class uttering some unpleasant statement. The professor also did not remind me of that out of her kindness and magnanimity. Likewise, most people don't like to ask for forgiveness thinking it as a below their dignity. So, many of us usually don't think of forgiving when it is most truly needed. Forgiving is not just forgetting, it is much more than that.

The incidence held around thirty years back has come back to my memory again. The two boys, whose mother was beaten by their father, could not forget the pain incurred to them when they were very young. Unfortunately, whenever they got a chance to return their hurt feelings, they did it by thrashing their father almost in the same manner he did to their mother. It is really very unfortunate that during such a crisis, we are unable to conceive any way out to solve the problem or to reach an amicable solution. To come out of the dilemma, one may seek different ways like going to movies, organising and joining parties, wasting time with the friends or indulging in drinks. It is just killing time to kill the pain. But the pain stays there hurting us severely. In fact, forgetting any feelings of hurt is very difficult. When we are unable to forget it, we feel that we are lost amid our dilemma. Consequently, we go on remembering the odd situation for long, staying disturbed and ready to take revenge. It is perhaps a very hard time of one's life when one is indulged with the thoughts of taking revenge. It is the moment when one is totally devoid of right thinking as the mind is loaded with the strong feelings of hate and revenge. Forgiving thus becomes very difficult. Therefore, there is no easy process to forgetting the ill-feelings. Some legendary examples may amplify such a situation clearly.

When Kauravas tried to undress Dropadi in public, the Pandavas, sitting there watching the Kauravas tearing her veils off her body and trying to make her totally naked in public, were unable to do anything at that time as they had lost her in gambling. But they could never forget that insult and their hurt remained unto them getting stronger as time passed by. Ultimately, they killed all the Kauravas in the battle and satisfied their hatred only after taking the revenge against them. It is a basic fact that most people are unable to forget their injuries and they go on planning how to take revenge.

I have already narrated the story of a senior security officer who said loudly thumping his chest that he knew more than what the other friend was narrating about the security department when we were discussing casually about the security of the country. A thoughtless talk usually takes one to a point where from there is hardly any return. The Great Buddha once warned us that we should not indulge in the arguments relating to the themes "Is there any heaven or hell? Where does man go after his death?" It is always judicious not to indulge in arguments that may end up in disharmony and create bitterness in our hearts. It would be prudent to stay away from such talks which lead us nowhere. Gradually, as we stay away from ill talks, we are led away from falling into the trap of retaliation. It helps us forgetting our hurt feelings and ultimately we forget all what has been delivered that far. So, forgetting is much more beneficial as it may suggest us to forgive also.

Without forgiveness one remains fastened to the person who inflicted any pain to us and we remain attached with bitterness. The moment we start thinking of 'forgiveness', our bitterness gradually gets melted. When we forgive, we become in a position to control our own feelings and become our own liberator.

Forgiving Implies Forgive Ourselves

Seeking forgiveness in other words is an excellent form of one's liberation from pain and self-interest. It is absolutely true spiritually too. When we forgive, we really don't forgive the other person, we forgive ourselves to get peace and liberation from the hurting feelings. When Buddha left his wife, Yashodhera and son, Rahul in the middle of the night sleeping, in order to venture in the world to attain freedom from the worldly attachments and to lead a life of a hermit, he could not forget the hurt he inflicted to them and to his parents as he went away without telling anyone. Even after he became a great saint and attained Enlightenment, the pain of hurting them remained within him. In order to let go that pain from his mind by asking her and his father their forgiveness, he went to see them when he camped with his retinue near Kapilabastu near his father's kingdom. He also met scores of people besides his father as well as Yashodhara and Rahul but did not utter a word when they complained about him to leave them in the middle of the night. Thus, by his visiting all these people he sought their forgiveness though never discussed it with them. (**Path of Dharma:** pp. 101-103)

The people, who reach such a great height in spirituality as the Buddha had attained, possess a different manner of seeking forgiveness. But they do seek it in some way to forget their ill treatment against others as it goes on reminding them who they hurt.

Most people who hurt others by their misdeeds never even think about how they torture others by their misdemeanour and go on celebrating their victory about their endeavour by defeating their opponent, but within themselves they always stay highly disturbed for causing pain to others. Even the murders who are put on the gallows when caught and punished to be hanged, during their final moments ask God's forgiveness against their ill deeds so that while they stay hanged and finally go, there remains no ill-will in their hearts.

Let us, therefore, never forget that forgiveness is the only right act to seek freedom from our pain that goes on and on hurting us and giving us the feelings of pain. The moment we sincerely seek forgiveness, we get relieved of the pain that had been there within us for so long. That is the only way to stay happy, at peace and to get salvation before we go finally. It also implies forgiving ourselves.

Archbishop Tutu rightly said: Forgiving is not forgetting; it's actually remembering—remembering not using your right to hit back (**Keep Calm and Pray**).

References

1. Desmond Tutu: (2014) **Why We Forgive:** July; Reader's Digest.
2. Hanson Dr. Rick (2009); **Buddha's Brain**; New York; New Harbinger Press Inc.
3. **Keep Calm and Pray** (2015) London: Andrew Mcmeel Publishing
4. Lisa TE Sonne (2013): **Buddha Meditations**;the Art of Letting Go; New York; Fall River Press.
5. Sharma A.P. (2007): **The Path of Dharma**; New Delhi; Pustak Mahal.
6. Sharma A.P. (2001) **Concept of Freedom: Krishnamurti**; Lincoln, iUniverse.Com
7. Sharma A.P. (2001) **Happiness is Divine**: Lincoln, iUniverse. Com
8. Sharma A.P. (2016) **Unparalleled Love**: Jaipur, Rudra, The Focus Company.
9. Strong, John S.(2001) **The Buddha: A short Biography**: England; One World Oxford.
10. Paramahansa Yogananda (1993) **Autobiography of a Yogi**; California: Self-Realisation Fellowship.